CONT

CW00853286

THE PONY CLUB PRINCE PHILII

THE PONY CLUB MOUNTED GA

PART 1 - GENERAL RULES OF M

PART 2 - RULES FOR MOUNTED GAMES COMPETITIONS...20

APPENDICES 71

THE PONY CLUB PRINCE PHILIP CUP OBJECTIVES

The Prince Philip Cup provides a Team competition requiring courage, determination and all-round riding ability on the part of the Team members, with careful and systematic training of their ponies.

The objective is to encourage a higher standard of riding throughout The Pony Club and to stimulate among the future generation a greater interest in riding as a sport and as a recreation.

This competition was designed for Teams of ordinary children on ordinary ponies and the practice by some Branches of retaining their own ponies to be used by successive Members of the Branch Team was certainly not envisaged by those who devised the Mounted Games concept. The Mounted Games Committee does not approve of this practice.

Where "Branch" is stated, this includes "Centres". All competitions are open to Branches and Centres. When a rule states District Commissioner, Centre Proprietor also applies.

RULES

These Rules are made by the Pony Club Mounted Games Committee in conjunction with other Pony Club Committees.

The Pony Club Office provides administrative support. Queries relating to these rules should be directed to the Mounted Games Sports Officer at The Pony Club Office at mountedgames@pcuk.org and the Mounted Games Chairman should be copied in when necessary.

Every eventuality cannot be provided for in these Rules. In any unforeseen or exceptional circumstances or any other issue in connection with Pony Club Mounted Games it is the duty of the relevant officials to make a decision in a sporting spirit and to approach as nearly as possible the intention of these Rules.

THE PONY CLUB MOUNTED GAMES COMMITTEE

Chairman

- Ian Mariner - mgchairman@pcuk.org (2027)

Committee Members

- Alison Bell (2027)
- Tracey Cooksley (2025)
- Pennie Drummond (2026)
- Vicki Dungait (2026)
- Marian Harding (2025)
- Brian Ross (2025)
- Catriona Willison (2027)
- Andrew James (Area Representative)
- Susan Goodridge (Area Representative)
- Marcus Capel (CEO) (2025)
- Carol Howsam (Co-opted) (2025)
- Caroline Barbour (Co-opted Youth Representation) (2025)

Sports Officer - mountedgames@pcuk.org

Area Coordinators:

- Area 1 - TBC
- Area 2 - TBC
- Area 3 - TBC
- Area 4 - Elaine Barker
- Area 5 - Clare Dawson
- Area 6 - TBC
- Area 7 - Caroline Chadwick
- Area 8 - Simon Duddy
- Area 9 - Caroline Queen
- Area 10 - Alison Davies
- Area 11 - Sheila Barbour
- Area 12 - Vicky Pattinson
- Area 13 - Philippa Westphal
- Area 14 - Nicola Way
- Area 15 - Mark Wilson
- Area 16 - TBC
- Area 17 - Biffy Booth
- Area 18 - Dennis Whitney
- Area 19 - May Wylie

Coordinators can be reached on the following email address:
mgcoordinator.areaX@pcuk.org replace X with the number of the Area you wish to contact e.g., Area 5 coordinator is mgcoordinator.area5@pcuk.org.

Thank you to all our Volunteers, Area Coordinators, and especially the Committee, for their hard work and commitment over The Pony Club year.

Area Coordinator is a voluntary role with the aim of giving as many Pony Club members as possible the opportunity to try the sport of Mounted Games. An Area MG Coordinator must be passionate about Mounted Games and knowledgeable about its rules. They should be over the age of 21 and have experience of being a team trainer, team manager, line steward, MG Committee member or DC. They can be an existing or previous member.

The Pony Club
Lowlands Equestrian Centre, Old Warwick Road, Warwick, CV35 7AX
Telephone: 02476 698300
pcuk.org

Health and Safety: safety@pcuk.org

NOTE: Rules which differ from those of 2024 appear in bold type and side-lined (as this note). Rules which require extra emphasis will also be in bold.

PART 1 - GENERAL RULES OF MOUNTED GAMES

1.   DRESS

New equipment is not required; however, all attire must be clean, neat, tidy, and safe. It is the competitor's responsibility to ensure their dress complies with the rules below, which prohibit the wearing of coloured silks and pom-poms, brightly coloured accessories, acrylics or gels, other false nails, certain types of jewellery, and sponsor advertising.

Hat silks are to be dark blue, black or brown in nature and must not have a logo larger than 4cm x 4cm. Contravention may incur disqualification.

Hats and white hat bands: The last rider in each team to go must wear a white hat band 5cm wide round their hat. They must be wearing the white hat band at the start of the race and throughout the race and must not enter the field of play until their turn, failure to do so will incur elimination.

a)   Hats and Hair:

Hair: Must be tied up and back (preferably in a hairnet) and securely, in a safe manner to reduce the risk of hair being caught and to prevent scalp injuries.

Hats: Members must always wear a protective hat when mounted. Only hats to the following specifications are acceptable at any Pony Club activity. The Pony Club is consistent with fellow BEF (British Equestrian) Member bodies in its Standards for Riding Hats. Individual sports may have additional requirements with regard to colour and type. It is strongly recommended that secondhand hats are not purchased.

The hat standards accepted as of 1st January 2025 are detailed in the table below:

Hat Standard	Safety Mark
Snell E2016 & 2021 with the official Snell label and number	
PAS 015: 2011 with BSI Kitemark or Inspec IC Mark	

(BS) EN 1384:2023 with BSI Kitemark or Inspec IC Mark	
VG1 with BSI Kitemark or Inspec IC Mark	
ASTM-F1163 2015 & 2023 with the SEI mark	
AS/NZS 3838, 2006 with SAI Global Mark	

Note: Some hats are dual-badged with different standards. If a hat contains at least one compliant hat standard it is deemed suitable to competition, even if it is additionally labelled with an older standard.

▸ For Mounted Games competitions, a jockey skull cap must be worn with no fixed peak, peak type extensions or noticeable protuberances above the eyes or to the front, and should have an even round or elliptical shape with a smooth or slightly abrasive surface, having no peak or peak type extensions. Noticeable protuberances above the eyes or to the front not greater than 5mm, smooth and rounded in nature are permitted. A removable hat cover with a light flexible peak may be used if required.

▸ No recording device is permitted (e.g. hat cameras) as they may have a negative effect on the performance of the hat in the event of a fall.

▸ The fit of the hat and the adjustment of the harness are as crucial as the quality. Members are advised to try several makes to find the best fit. The hat should not move on the head when the head is tipped forward. The Pony Club recommends you visit a qualified BETA (British Equestrian Trade Association) fitter.

▸ Hats must be replaced after a severe impact as subsequent protection will be significantly reduced. Hats deteriorate with age and should be replaced after three to five years depending upon the amount of use.

▸ Hats must be worn at all times (including at prize-giving) when mounted with a chinstrap fastened and adjusted so as to prevent movement of the hat in the event of a fall.

▶ For Mounted Games: hat covers, if applicable, shall be dark blue, black or brown only.

▶ The Official Steward / Organiser may, at their discretion, eliminate a competitor riding in the area of the competition without a hat or with the chinstrap unfastened or with a hat that does not comply with these standards.

Hat Checks and Tagging

The Pony Club and its Branches and Centres will appoint Officials, who are familiar with The Pony Club hat rule, to carry out hat checks and tag each hat that complies with the requirements set out in the hat rule with an Pony Club hat tag. Hats fitted with a Pony Club, British Eventing (BE) or British Riding Club (BRC) hat tag will not need to be checked on subsequent occasions. However, the Pony Club reserves the right to randomly spot check any hat regardless of whether it is already tagged.

Tagging is an external verification of the internal label and indicates that a hat meets the accepted standards. The tag does NOT imply any check of the fit and condition of the hat has been undertaken. It is considered to be the responsibility of the Member's parent(s) / guardian(s) to ensure that their hat complies with the required standards and is tagged before they go to any Pony Club event. Also, they are responsible for ensuring that the manufacturer's guidelines with regard to fit and replacement are followed.

For further information on hat standards, testing and fitting, please refer to the British Equestrian Trade Association (BETA) website: British Equestrian Trade Association - Safety and your head (beta-uk.org)

b)   Body Protectors:

A body protectors is compulsory for all Pony Club Cross Country riding (including Arena Eventing) and Pony Racing activities whether it be training or competition. A body protector for these activities must meet BETA 2018 Level 3 Standard (blue and black label).

For general use, the responsibility for choosing body protectors and the decision as to their use must rest with Members and their parents. It is recommended that a rider's body protector should not be more than

2% of their body weight. When worn, body protectors must fit correctly, be comfortable and must not restrict movement. BETA recommends body protectors are replaced at least every three to five years, after which the impact absorption properties of the foam may have started to decline.

Air Jackets

It is strongly recommended that air jackets are NOT worn for Mounted Games activities due to frequent mounting and dismounting.

c)   Jodhpurs/Riding Tights: Jodhpurs/riding tights, including any visible logos or brand names, must be of a single colour. For National Trials, RWHS, and HOYS, riders must wear cream or beige jodhpurs or riding tights. At all other levels, legwear must be black, cream, or beige, and there must be uniformity across the team, including the 6th member. White or other coloured jodhpurs/riding tights are not allowed. Belts may be worn.

d)   Shirts: White shirts with long sleeves (which are not to be rolled up) and Pony Club ties. In cold or wet weather white sweatshirts and/or colourless transparent or white waterproof garments with long sleeves may be worn over the white shirt. At Area Competitions, Teams will wear their Branch Centre coloured bibs over their shirts or sweatshirts. Bibs may be provided for Teams competing at Zone Finals and The Pony Club Championships if there is a clash of colours

e)   Footwear: Only standard riding or jodhpur boots with a well- defined square cut heel may be worn. Plain black or brown half chaps maybe worn with jodhpur boots of the same colour. Tassels and fringes are not allowed. No other footwear will be permitted, including wellington boots, yard boots, country boots, "muckers" or trainers. Boots with interlocking treads are not permitted, nor are the boots or treads individually. Laces on boots must be taped.

Stirrups should be of the correct size to suit the rider's boots (see Rule 2(b))

f)   Badges: These are optional. If worn, they should be of cloth, not metal, and may be sewn on to the bib.

g)   Jewellery: the wearing of any sort of jewellery when handling or riding a horse/pony is not recommended and if done at any Pony Club activity, is done at the risk of the member/their parent/guardian. However, to stop any risk of injury, necklaces and bracelets (other than medical bracelets) must be removed, as must larger and more pendulous pieces of jewellery (including those attached to piercings) which create a risk of injury to the body part through which they are secured.

h)   **Whips and spurs:** are not allowed.

i)   **Electronic Devices:** (i.e. headphones, mobile phones etc. enabling another person to communicate with the rider) are not allowed whilst the rider is competing. No recording device is permitted. (e.g. head/bridle cameras etc.)

j)   **Acrylics/gels** and other false nails are not allowed.

k)   **Sponsor Advertising:** is not allowed on rider's dress, numnahs and saddlery unless they have been presented at The Pony Club Championships in the current or previous years.

2. SADDLERY

The Pony Club prefers competitors to use plain saddlery, but it is not compulsory. New equipment is not expected, but what is worn must be clean, neat and tidy and safe.

Any misuse of a bit or bridle will be reported to the District Commissioner, Area Representative and the Training Chairman. Any reported riders will be recorded, monitored or maybe disqualified.

Badly fitting or unsafe tack, or saddles that are down on the withers when the rider is mounted, will result in the disqualification of that competitor, unless they decide to re- present in the correct saddlery/equipment to the satisfaction of the Official Steward, before the start of the competition.

No item of tack may be used for any other purpose, or in any other way than the one for which it was designed and intended, e.g. Running Martingales may not be used as Standing Martingales.

Saddlery which is not allowed in the Games may not be worn on the day of competition. Any Team/Individual found to have changed, or altered the

fitting of, an item of Tack/Clothing, without permission, may be penalised by disqualification from the competition.

The Official Steward has absolute discretion in ruling on these matters.

a)   **Saddles:** Must be made on a conventional general-purpose tree Racing saddles measuring less than 16 inches (40.6cm) in length (i.e. from front arch to cantle) and weighing less than 5lb (2.8kg) are NOT permitted.

The use of Pad Saddles is only permitted on small native type ponies, with the written permission of the DC and the agreement of the Official Steward Where handles cannot be removed, these must be taped up. If the stirrup bars have safety clips, they must be in a downward position. Pad saddles that do not have stirrup bars that can remain open must be used with stirrups designed to ensure the easy release of the foot. These stirrups must also fully comply with all requirements outlined in rule b).

b) **Stirrups:** Stirrups should be of the correct size to suit the rider's boots. They must have 7mm (¼") clearance on either side of the boot. To find this measurement, tack checkers should move the foot across to one side of the stirrup, with the widest part of the foot on the tread. From the side of the boot to the edge of the stirrup should not be less than 14mm.

There are now many types of stirrups marketed as 'safety stirrups'. All riders must ensure that their stirrups are suitable for the type of footwear they are wearing and the activities in which they are taking part and that the stirrup leathers are in good condition.

There are no prescribed weight limits on metal stirrups, however with the advent of stirrups of other materials, weight limits are frequently given by manufacturers. Any person buying these stirrups, should comply with weight limits defined on the box or attached information leaflets. Neither the feet nor the stirrup leathers or irons, may be attached to the girth, nor the feet attached to the stirrup irons.

It is strongly recommended that the design of the stirrup chosen allows the foot to be released easily in the event of a rider fall. Specific rules for individual sports can be found in the respective sports rulebooks.

Particular focus should be on ensuring that the boot and stirrup are the correct size for the rider taking part and used in line with the manufacturer's guidance.

For the avoidance of doubt, at Pony Club events:

▸ stirrups which connect the boot and the stirrup magnetically are not allowed
▸ Interlocking boot soles and stirrup treads are not allowed
▸ Bostock & Free Jump stirrups are not allowed at Pony Club Mounted Games events.
▸ Stirrups which include metal/metal type treads, including but not limited to those with protruding spikes and / or perforated grip features are NOT permitted.

c) **Girths:** White, navy blue, brown or black girths with two separate buckles. Humane girths are not allowed as they pose an increased risk as many common designs may have complete girth failure if a single strap was to break.

d) **Numnahs / Saddle Cloths:** Any solid colour is permitted. Contrasting piping is permitted. Branch logos are allowed when competing for the Branch; logos must not exceed 200 sq. cm. This does not preclude the wearing of clothing for horses or riders that has been presented by sponsors of The Pony Club Championships in the current or previous years.

e) **Bridles:** Plain black or brown leather. Micklem bridles are permitted (with rings taped). Bitless bridles are not allowed.

f) **Reins:** For safety reasons, knotted reins must be attached to the bit by a leather buckle or billet. Large loops of rein behind the knot are not safe. This can be avoided by undoing the buckle or by taping the looped reins together. Any plain, solid-coloured reins are permitted for Mounted Games. Bridge/Market Harborough/Balance Support reins are not permitted.

g) **Grass Reins:** (Allowed for Junior and Novice Junior competitions only)

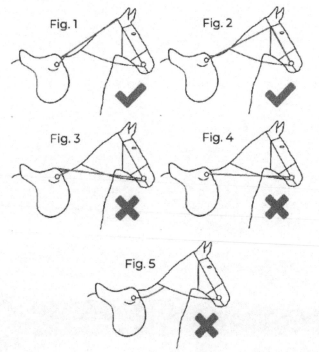

Only those grass reins shown in diagrams 1 and 2 are permitted. Grass reins must be fitted to allow and not restrict the normal head position of the pony. The rein length must be sufficient to allow the pony to stretch over a small fence.

Grass reins may be leather or synthetic material, if synthetic then a break point of leather or other suitable material must be included.

h)   Browbands: coloured are permitted.

i)   Nosebands: Only one noseband is permitted – Cavesson, Drop, Grackle or Flash unless using a Standing martingale with a drop or grackle noseband in which case the addition of a cavesson is allowed. Nosebands must not incorporate chain or rope.

Note: Sheepskin nosebands/blinkers or any attachments to the pony or bridle which may affect the animal's field of vision are NOT permitted.

j)   Martingales: Irish, Bib, Running, Standing (with or without elastic), only one of which may be worn at any time. Standing Martingales may be attached only to a Cavesson Noseband or the Cavesson portion of a 'Flash' noseband fitted above the bit. Five-point breast plates are allowed.

Vaulting, balance, neck straps/collars are NOT permitted.

k)   Bandages/Boots: Should only be worn where necessary and not for decoration. They must be of uniform colour and correctly fitted.

l)   Hoof Boots: are not allowed.

m)   Studs: The use of Studs is not recommended unless absolutely necessary. If worn, road studs may be used. In adverse weather conditions the studs illustrated below may be used.

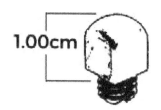
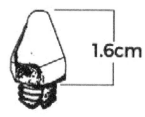

n)   Fly hoods, ear plugs and ear covers: Are NOT permitted

o)   Nose nets are permitted: Nose nets must cover the nose only leaving the mouth and bit visible.

p)   Clips on saddlery are not permitted anywhere, unless taped over

q) **Bits:** The bit must be a plain snaffle with a straight bar, single or double joint in the middle. The mouthpiece must be smooth all round. Bits of nylon or other synthetic material are permitted, should be black, brown or white and must be used in their manufactured condition without any addition to/or on any part. Bit Guards must be black, white or brown and smooth on both sides.

Thin Bits – In the opinion of the Chief Steward and the Tack Officials, bits deemed to be excessively thin in the mouthpiece will not be accepted.

Hanging Snaffle bits must be of a standard type. Dr Bristol and Fulmer bits are not allowed.

The only bits permitted for use at Area level and above are those illustrated below or any combination of the mouthpieces, rings or cheeks.

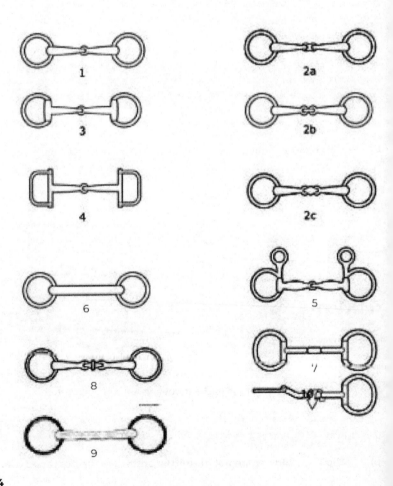

- ▶ 1.   Loose ring snaffle
- ▶ 2.a   Snaffle with double-jointed mouthpiece (French link)
- ▶ 2.b   Snaffle with double-jointed mouthpiece
- ▶ 2.c   Snaffle with double-jointed mouthpiece with Lozenge
- ▶ 3.   Egg-butt snaffle
- ▶ 4.   Racing snaffle D-ring
- ▶ 5.   Hanging cheek snaffle (standard type only)
- ▶ 6.   Straight bar snaffle. Permitted also with Mullen mouth and egg butt rings.
- ▶ 7.   Snaffle with rotating mouthpiece
- ▶ 8.   Snaffle with rotating middle piece
- ▶ 9.   Un-jointed wavy snaffle (plastic or rubber only)

3.   PONIES AND VACCINATIONS

Must be sound and well shod, or with their feet properly dressed.

Ponies must be groomed and well trimmed, and manes and tails must not be plaited. Ponies that are infirm through old age, ill, thin or lame or are a danger to their riders or others are unacceptable. Veterinary letters regarding the soundness/condition of a pony will NOT be accepted.

At Area Competitions and Zone Finals a pony may compete in the PPC, Novice Juniors, Juniors and Pairs if in the opinion of the DC/Centre Proprietor and the owner that the pony is fit enough and used in the appropriate number of races.

Any pony that becomes distressed may be withdrawn from the competition at the discretion of the Official Steward.

THE PONY CLUB VACCINATION RULES

A valid passport and vaccination record:

- ▶   must accompany the horse/pony to all events
- ▶   must be available for inspection by the event officials
- ▶   must be produced on request at any other time during the event

All ponies/horses must be compliant with the current Pony Club minimum vaccination requirements - please see the website for the current rule.

Note: Events that are held at other venues may be subject to additional specific rules. For example, any horse/pony entering a Licensed Racecourse Property must comply with the Vaccination requirements as set by the British Horseracing Authority. Similar restrictions apply in the cases of certain polo venues. If you are intending to compete under FEI Rules you will need to ensure you are compliant with those Rules.

4.   ACTION AFTER A FALL

As a training organisation, The Pony Club prioritises the welfare of riders and the safety of all participants and spectators.

A rider must not remount after a fall if there is any doubt regarding their fitness, regardless of the wishes of parents, trainers, or others. Further participation may only occur following an examination by a medical professional.

In the event of a rider fall:

a)   Any competitor who suffers a serious fall or injury anywhere on the competition site MUST see medical personnel on the day and must be declared fit to ride before mounting any other pony.

b)   If a rider appears injured, the Official Steward has the authority to stop the race. All Line Stewards will raise their boards in response.

c)   The nearest Official (usually the Line Steward) will immediately attend to the rider and, if necessary, summon additional help through the Official Steward.

d)   When a race is stopped due to injury, it will be re-run. However, the Team or the Pair of the fallen rider may not participate in the re-run. Any Team or Pair that completed the race prior to the incident will retain their final placing. Any Team or Pair that has not completed will re-run.

NB: Under no circumstances may parents or first aiders enter the active field of play whilst the race is still in, as this poses a risk of further injury to themselves or others.

5.   HEAD INJURY AND CONCUSSION

If a person is diagnosed with a concussion, they must not ride or take part in any Pony Club organised activity that involves close contact/handling or riding of horses or ponies for 21 days. This may need to be extended if symptoms persist, on the advice of the treating doctor. All concussion must be reported to Head Office using the online accident report form or by email if it occurred outside of The Pony Club. Concussion advice should be followed without exception.

Head injuries and concussion can be very serious and life changing. Serious head injuries are usually obvious, but concussion can be very subtle. It may not be immediately apparent but should be taken very seriously. Recovery from concussion should be managed carefully.

This rule should be read in conjunction with:

▸ The Pony Club Concussion Advice

▸ UK Government Concussion Guidelines

Please contact safety@pcuk.org for further support and advice.

6.   MEDICAL SUSPENSION

If a Member has been suspended from taking part in any activity/ competition/sport for medical reasons, this suspension must apply to all Pony Club activities until such time the Member is passed fit by a medical professional to take part. It is the Member and parent/guardian's responsibility to ensure this rule is adhered to.

Medical letters are required, following a suspension for medical reasons, to allow a Member to take part in any activity again. The letter should be issued by the either the hospital or specialist(s) involved in treating the injury, where appropriate.

7.   UNSEEMLY BEHAVIOUR

Unseemly behaviour on the part of riders, Team officials, or Team supporters will be reported as soon as possible by the Official to The Pony Club Office, and they may be penalised by disqualification of the Branch(es) concerned for a period up to three years. Any competitor who in the opinion of the Official Steward, or Organiser, has been extremely rude or aggressive towards any officials at a competition, or who has behaved in an aggressive or unfair manner to their horse may be disqualified.

8.   PERFORMANCE-ENHANCING DRUGS

All performance-enhancing drugs are strictly forbidden and The Pony Club supports 100% clean sport.

a) Equine – Controlled Medication

It is essential for the welfare of a horse/pony that appropriate veterinary treatment is given if and when required. Some medication, however, may mask an underlying health problem so horses and ponies should not take part in training or competition when taking such medication and any Therapeutic Use Exemptions (TUE) should be confirmed in writing by a Vet.

b) Human

Performance-enhancing drugs are forbidden. The Pony Club supports the approach taken by the UK Anti-Doping Agency in providing clean sport. The Pony Club disciplinary procedures would be used in cases where doping may be suspected including reporting to the UK Anti-Doping Agency.

c) Testing

All competitors should be aware that random samples may be taken for testing from both themselves and/or their horse/pony. The protocol used will be that of the relevant adult discipline.

Competitors and their horses/ponies at national or international level may be subject to blood tests in line with the Sports Council Policy on illegal and prescribed substances. All young people competing at these levels should be made aware of this

d) Reporting

i) Anyone who has reasonable grounds for suspecting that a Member is using or selling an illegal substance must report their concerns to the District Commissioner/Centre Proprietor as soon as practicable. If there is an immediate risk to the health, safety or welfare of one or more Members then the Police must be informed as soon as possible. The person reporting their concerns must ensure that any material evidence is retained and should not influence any police investigation.

ii) Upon receiving a report of suspected use or selling of an illegal substance the District Commissioner/Centre Proprietor should carry out an immediate investigation of the incident and the circumstances in which it occurred, and then decide upon the appropriate action to be taken. This will include:

- ▶ Informing the Member's parents/guardians
- ▶ Informing The Pony Club Area Representative who in turn will inform The Pony Club Office
- ▶ Informing the Police
- ▶ Suspending the Member concerned while investigations are completed
- ▶ Awaiting the completion of Police investigations and actions

9.   DISQUALIFICATION

Rough or dangerous riding, deliberate interference, unseemly behaviour, or unauthorised changes of tack, etc., may be penalised by disqualification of the rider or team from the next race, the event concerned or the whole competition, at the discretion of the Official Steward, and reported to the Mounted Games Committee, District Commissioner / Centre Proprietor, Area Representative and the Training Chairman. Any reported riders will be recorded and monitored.

10.   SPONSORSHIP

In the case of horses, riders and owners, no form of advertising – and this includes a sponsor's name - may appear on the competitor's or horse's clothing and equipment at any Pony Club competition. This does not preclude the wearing of clothing for horses and riders that has been presented by sponsors of The Pony Club Championships in the current or previous years.

11.   INSURANCE

The Pony Club 'Public and Products Liability Insurance' Policy includes cover for all the official Area Competitions and the Championships. Details of this insurance are available on The Pony Club website.

In the event of any accident, loss or damage occurring to a third party or to the property of a third party (including the general public and competitors) no liability should be admitted, and full details should be sent at once to The Pony Club Office.

The following statements should be included in all event schedules:

HEALTH & SAFETY

Organisers of this event have taken reasonable precautions to ensure the health and safety of everyone present. For these measures to be effective, everyone must take all reasonable precautions to avoid and prevent accidents occurring and must obey the instructions of the organisers and all the officials and stewards.

LEGAL LIABILITY

Save for the death or personal injury caused by the negligence of the organisers, or anyone for whom they are in law responsible, neither the organisers of this event or The Pony Club nor any agent, employee or representative of these bodies, nor the landlord or their tenant, accepts any liability for any accident, loss, damage, injury or illness to horses, owners, riders, spectators, land, cars, their contents and accessories, or any other person or property whatsoever. Entries are only accepted on this basis.

PART 2 - RULES FOR MOUNTED GAMES COMPETITIONS

The competitions will be run in stages. The first will be the Area Competitions to be completed by **1st June 2025**. The second will be the Zone Finals, the third stage will be at The Pony Club Championships. The winning Senior Team from each Zone competition will qualify for HOYS and will not compete at the Championships. The runners-up and the winning Senior Team at the Championships will also qualify for HOYS.

Format of all competitions will be run as Seniors followed by Juniors and then the Pairs. Novices can be run at Area level subject to Teams being available and can be run sometime during the day as arranged by the organising Branch.

12. PRINCE PHILIP CUP (SENIOR) TEAMS

The full Branch/Centre team consists of:

a) Four or Five riders who must be active Members of the stated Branch of The Pony Club. All Team members must hold valid membership throughout all stages of each competition.

Members must not have attained their 15th birthday prior to the beginning of the current calendar year (i.e. they must have been born in the year 2010 or later).

Note: Some games require a fifth member (on foot) to hold equipment. At HOYS, some games require five riders and five ponies.

b) A sixth member may be nominated; they may only be used to hold equipment in races where all five take part, and then only in the case of injury to one of the other Team members. The sixth member must be eligible under the rules of the competition, named on the declaration form and attend the turnout inspection correctly dressed for the competition. The declared sixth member for a Senior Team may be a Junior, even if there are already two Juniors forming part of that Senior Team. All sixth member must also be free from any Branch transfer as described in Rule 14.

c) Four or five ponies, at least four years old and not exceeding 148 cm, are permitted. A horse or pony is deemed to reach the age of 1 on the 1st of January following the date of foaling and is considered a year older on each successive 1st of January.

d)   Height/weight

▸   A rider weighing over 54kg may not ride a pony 128cm or under.
▸   A rider weighing over 60kg may not ride a pony 133cm or under.
▸   A rider weighing over 66kg may not ride a pony 138cm or under.

Riders will be weighed dressed to compete, including helmet and boots.

If any Team Member changes to a different pony during the competition, the same height/weight rules apply.

Note: There is no upper rider weight limit, however, the Mounted Games Committee will monitor riders and ponies and will have the discretion to disqualify any rider considered to be unsuitably mounted.

e)   Pony measurement is conducted without shoes (1¼ cm is deducted when the pony is shod). Official Joint Measurement Board Ltd height certificates will be accepted (in accordance with current JMB rules).

f)   Normally four riders and ponies take part in each event, so the riders and/or ponies may be changed for the different events. The fifth rider and/or pony may be substituted for the final in any race.

g)   Members and ponies of Teams and Pairs may be changed between the Area competition, Zone Finals, The Pony Club Championships and HOYS.

h)   No pony or rider can compete for more than one Branch in a single calendar year.

i)   An adult or senior member of the Branch aged 18 or over will be appointed as the Team Trainer. Their duties include taking charge of the Team outside the arena and sending the Team in immediately when called. The Team Trainer may not enter the field of play to assist or coach the Team. Coaching is only allowed from the rear of the arena or from the trainers track and not from the side or top of the arena.

13.   COMBINED TEAMS

a)   If a Branch has members who are not part of a Branch Team, those members may be grouped with members from other Branches within the same Area, who are also not part of a Branch Team, to form a Combined Team.

b)   The formation of a Combined Team requires prior permission from all relevant District Commissioners and the Area Representative.

c) A Combined Team must practise together at least once before the Area Competition. The relevant District Commissioners must nominate a Team Trainer for the team and an additional individual responsible for the overall management of the Combined Team.

d) At the discretion of the Mounted Games Committee, a Combined Team may be permitted to advance to the Zone Finals, but no further. This is contingent upon confirmation from all DCs and the AR that the Combined Team was formed according to Rule 13(a). The participation of Combined Teams in the Area Competition will count towards the total number of qualifying teams from the Area to the Zone.

Combined Teams will be reviewed annually, and Branches will be encouraged to recruit new members to compete as part of a Branch Team.

14. TRANSFER OF MEMBERS

a) Members wishing to transfer between Branches to compete in Mounted Games are actively discouraged from doing so, as this is considered not to be in the best interests of The Pony Club and the sport of Mounted Games.

b) Any member who transfers from one Branch to another will be ineligible to represent their new Branch in the Senior Prince Philip Cup Competition at the Area, Zone, The Pony Club Championships, and Horse of the Year Show for a period of 14 months from the date of their transfer. This ineligibility applies even if a Junior rider becomes a Senior rider during this period.

c) Any member who transfers from one Branch to another will be ineligible for selection to represent their new Branch at any National Trial for the Royal Windsor Horse Show or other International competitions for a period of 14 months from the date of their transfer.

d) Any member who is ineligible under Rule 14(b) to represent their Branch at an Area Competition shall also be ineligible to compete in the later stages of the Prince Philip Cup Competition during that year.

NB: No part of this rule 14 applies to the Junior Competition, the Pairs competition, Friendly competitions, County Shows, External Events, and Exhibitions.

A transfer between Branches includes the transfer from Centre Plus to Branch membership.

15.   AREA COMPETITIONS

Area Competitions must be held no later than **1st June 2025** at venues agreed to by Area Representatives. They will be organised solely by the Branch hosting the event, including the collection of entry forms and fees. All Teams must compete in their own Area Competition. Under normal circumstances, no more than six Teams may compete in any heat or final; however, if entries warrant, seven Teams may run. The Organiser must consult the Official Steward before this is implemented and receive their permission.

Where there are 18 Teams or fewer, each game will consist of 3 heats and a final of 6 Teams. Where there are 12 Teams or fewer, each game will consist of 2 heats and a final of 6 Teams. Where there are 7 Teams or fewer, Teams can be run in 1 heat.

Semi-finals must not be run unless there are more than 18 Teams entered.

In Areas where more than 18 Teams are entered, at the discretion of the Organiser and the Official Steward, the Competition may be divided into two separate sections, normally in the morning and afternoon. The Area Organiser will notify the Teams when they are to compete.

It is recommended that the Tack & Turnout Inspection for Teams competing in the afternoon section can be held during the end of the morning competition.

At each Area Competition, the Teams will compete against each other in eight races for Seniors and Pairs, and seven races for the Junior competition as listed in this Rulebook.

a)   Declarations:

Forms are available for download from the Resource Hub on the website. On the day of the competition, Teams must submit a Declaration Form to the Organiser/Official Steward. This form must include the names and PELHAM membership numbers of the Team members, details of their ponies (including passport numbers), and the PELHAM Coach Accreditation number of the Team Trainer.

DCs must sign the Declaration Form only when it has been fully completed.

If a Team fails to produce a valid and accurate Declaration Form and a breach of eligibility is later discovered, the Team may be disqualified.

Invitations to Zones and The Pony Club Championships will be sent using the contact details provided on the Declaration Form, so please ensure they are clearly printed. Only the declared members and ponies are eligible to compete on the day.

If required, Reasonable Adjustment Application (RAA) forms must be submitted along with the member's Personal Profile to the organiser, with the Mounted Games Chairman copied in, at least two weeks before the competition. If submitted after this deadline, there is no guarantee the adjustment can or will be applied.

b) **Entries:** Each Branch may enter any number of Teams for all Area Competitions.

c) **Scoring:** Every Team completing a heat will score one point. In the Final, the winning Team will score the same number of points as the number of Teams competing.

Teams eliminated in a heat will score NO points.

Teams eliminated in a Final will score NO points (but will retain the point from their heat).

If the competition is run without the need of heats and finals, then all heats will be scored based on the number of teams taking part.

d) **Ties:** In the case of a draw for qualifying places from a heat to a final, only the Teams concerned will re-run the race.

In the event of a tie in a final, the points will be divided between the Teams involved. If there is a draw for overall placings at an event, the Teams will compete in a tie-break race.

e) **Qualifiers:**

▶ In Area Competitions where 18 or more Teams compete in each competition on the day, six Teams qualify for the Zone Finals.

▶ In Areas where 15-17 Teams compete, five Teams will qualify.

▶ In Areas where 11-14 Teams compete, four Teams will qualify.

▶ In Areas where 8-10 Teams compete, three Teams will qualify.

▶ In Areas where fewer than 8 Teams compete, two Teams will qualify.

Once all 19 Area Competitions are completed, additional qualifications may be awarded to Teams that did not qualify through the automatic qualification requirements.

This process is designed to ensure that each Zone competition has between 14 and 21 Teams competing in the Senior, Junior, and Pairs competitions. Additional qualifications are determined by averaging the scores from each Area competition to ensure comparability across Areas. The highest scoring Teams that have not already qualified may receive additional qualifications to compete at the Zone Finals if there are available spots.

If a Team withdraws from the Zone Finals, their place will be offered to the next highest placed Team from the same Area competition.

f)   Zone Finals: Four Zone Finals will be arranged to take place in July. At Zone Finals, Teams will compete against each other in 10 Races (8 for Juniors) and Finals as listed in this Rulebook.

The winning Team from each Zone Final will qualify for the Horse of the Year Show (HOYS).

g)   Runners-up Competition: Branches placed 2nd to 7th at each Zone Final will compete for the final two HOYS places at The Pony Club Championships. Scoring heats may be used in the initial phase of the competition.

Any rider or pony that competed in a Branch Team which qualified for HOYS at Zone Finals in the current year may not compete again in the Senior Runners-Up competitions at The Pony Club Championships.

▸   Runners-up Competition – Sunday 10th August 2025

h)   Intermediate Championship: Teams placed 8th to 10th at each Zone Final, and therefore not qualifying for Senior Runners-Up Competition at the Championships will be invited to the Intermediate Championships at The Pony Club Championships in August.

Any rider or pony that competed in a Branch Team which qualified for HOYS or that competes in The Pony Club Mounted Games Senior Runners-up competitions in the current year, cannot also compete at Intermediate Championships at The Pony Club Championships.

Due to the International Mounted Games Exchange competition to be held on the 9th of August 2025, this competition will be scoring heats only.

▸   Intermediate Championship – Saturday 9th August 2025

16.   JUNIOR COMPETITION

a)   Format: A three-round competition consisting of Area qualifiers and Junior Zone Finals to be held in conjunction with the present Prince

Philip Cup Senior Competitions at these levels and a National Final at The Pony Club Championships.

b)   **Teams:** As Prince Philip Cup Competition Rules, except:

i.   Riders must not have attained their 11th birthday prior to the beginning of the current calendar year (i.e. born in the year of 2014 or after).

ii.   Members and ponies eligible for a Junior Team may contribute to the numbers in a Prince Philip Cup Senior Team, with a maximum of two Members and/or two ponies allowed. For example, two Members and/or ponies from a Junior Team can compete in a Senior A Team, and an additional two Members and/or ponies from the same Junior Team can compete in a Senior B Team. This rule does not apply to a Junior Member who serves as the non-riding sixth Member in a Prince Philip Cup Team.

c)   **Area Competitions:** As for Prince Philip Cup Competition Rules.

i.   Should an Area wish to hold its Area Junior Competition separately from its Area Prince Philip Cup event, this is permitted with the agreement of the Area Representative and the Official Steward.

ii.   At all events, the Prince Philip Cup Competition will be run first.

d)   **Junior Zone Finals:** Four Zone Finals will take place in conjunction with the Prince Philip Cup Zone Finals. Each Junior Zone Final will usually consist of 14 to 21 Teams.

e)   **National Final – held at The Pony Club National Championships**

The top seven Teams from each of the Zones will compete in the National Junior Final. Full details of this competition will be handed to the qualifying Teams at their Zone Final.

▸   Junior Championships – Friday 8th August 2025

17.   PAIRS COMPETITION

▸   Members must have attained their 11th birthday before the beginning of the current calendar year and must not have reached their 19th birthday by the same date.
▸   Members can compete in Pairs either from the same Branch or as a mix of two Branches, provided both are within the same Area.
▸   If a Branch has two eligible members, they must compete as a Pair within that Branch. Single members may combine with a single member from another Branch in the same Area to form a Mixed Pair.

- Mixed Pairs will be designated using the format 'Branch A/Branch B'.
- Members may compete in both the Pairs Competition and the Prince Philip Cup Competition.
- Both members and ponies may be substituted as needed.
- Height and weight rules will follow those outlined in the Prince Philip Cup and Junior competitions.
- All heats will be scored individually, and there will be no finals. The results will be based on the total points scored from heats.
- Coloured hat bands or hat silks may be used in the Pairs Competition. Each lane will have a designated hat silk colour, and the last rider in the pair competing in that lane will receive the specific-coloured hat silk (e.g., if lane 3 is red, the last rider in each pair competing in lane 3 will wear a red hat silk). There is no requirement to wear a white hat band when using coloured hat silks.
- If more than seven pairs are entered, heats will be run and scored, with the winning Pair receiving points equivalent to the number of Pairs competing in the largest heat.
- **White base layers may be worn by both riders with their coloured bibs on top.**

Qualifiers (Area Competitions):
- Where 18 or more Pairs compete on the day 6 Pairs will qualify
- Where 15-17 Pairs compete on the day 5 Pairs will qualify
- Where 11-14 Pairs compete on the day 4 Pairs will qualify
- Where 8-10 Pairs compete on the day 3 Pairs will qualify
- Where fewer than 8 Pairs compete, 2 Pairs will qualify

Depending on the number of Pairs Teams competing at Area Competitions additional qualifying places may be allocated to make up the number competing at Zone Finals at the discretion of the Mounted Games Committee.

Notes for Pairs Competitions:
- Pairs qualify from Area to Zone to Championships
- The top seven Pairs from each of the Zones will compete in the Pairs Final. Full details of this competition will be given to the qualifying Pairs at their Zone Final.

Pairs Final – held at The Pony Club National Championships Saturday 9th August 2025

Games: The games rules will follow the Area/Zone/Championship rules adapted to suit Pairs.

18.   GUIDELINES FOR NOVICE COMPETITIONS

The Novice Competition is an introductory step for children wishing to compete in Area Pony Club Mounted Games. Its aim is to encourage participation and achievement through support and simplified races, with Area Coordinators available for assistance.

Competitions may be organised as lead rein events, allowing children who demonstrate competence to progress to Junior/Senior Mounted Games Teams. The focus is on creating a safe and enjoyable environment.

Novice competitions can be integrated into Branch-friendly events, using the same arena and equipment. To help children learn Mounted Games rules, competitions should follow The Pony Club Mounted Games Rulebook, with the following additional guidelines:

This competition is for Members learning the skills and rules of Pony Club Mounted Games, who may require a leader. Suggested games are listed in the Resource Hub on the pcuk.org website to aid skill development for future competitions.

Ponies may be ridden in any standard riding bit with a single rein, excluding English gags and bitless bridles (grass reins are permitted).

Trainers may accompany their Teams and guide Members during races.

Ponies may be led, but the leader can only assist for safety reasons.

Children should correct mistakes, dismounting, if necessary, but may receive assistance from the leader to remount if they are too small.

The safety of children and ponies is paramount; trainers and District Commissioners must ensure all participants are suitably mounted.

It is recommended that heats be scored based on placings rather than as separate heats and finals.

Members confidently competing at the Novice level should be encouraged to participate in Area Competitions.

19.   FRIENDLY BRANCH COMPETITIONS AND EXTERNAL EVENTS

a)   Branch Friendly Competitions

Branches may organise Friendly Mounted Games competitions for all ages and abilities, including Teams, Pairs, and individuals (including lead reins).

Combined Teams are permitted with the agreement of the organising Branch.

All Branch Friendly Mounted Games competitions must be publicised on the Pony Club website.

While the Mounted Games Rulebook provides a framework for these competitions, the format and choice of games should reflect the age, competence, size, and experience of the Members and ponies involved.

All Friendly Games Competitions should be organised by a Branch with the knowledge and permission of the District Commissioner and Branch Committee. Notice should also be given to the Area Representative and/or the local Member of the Mounted Games Committee or Area Coordinator.

The guidelines for running Area Competitions should be considered best practice for organising Friendly Competitions; however, there will be no involvement from Head Office. Therefore, the appointment of an Official Steward, Line Stewards, the supply of rosettes, and funding will be the sole responsibility of the organising Branch.

The importance of appointing experienced officials cannot be overstated.

In addition to safety guidelines for Area Competitions, general health, safety, and risk assessment principles apply to all Branch events, including Friendly Competitions. The Risk Assessment conducted by the organising Branch will be crucial in determining the appropriate level of First Aid cover.

b)   External Events: County Shows, Trade Shows, or other Major Equestrian Events

Pony Club Mounted Games Team Competitions may occasionally take place outside the Branch network, typically at shows or other major equestrian events, and these events may be by invitation only.

Planned attendance at external events must be notified to The Pony Club Office/Area Representative, and their permission may be required. All County Shows, Trade Shows, and other major equine events must be publicised on the Pony Club website.

Combined Teams may be invited to participate if additional numbers are needed. A Pony Club Official must be appointed to oversee the event and assume overall responsibility.

The appointed Pony Club Official must conduct a thorough Risk Assessment in accordance with The Pony Club guidelines and should request a copy of the event's own Risk Assessment. These assessments must cover all relevant aspects, including the arena, collecting ring, horse walks, overnight stays, penning, and practice areas.

Additionally, the Pony Club Official is required to record and report any accidents or incidents to The Pony Club Office, if not done so by the organising Branch. Any Health and Safety concerns that Organisers have prior to, during, or after the event should be raised directly with the office.

c)   Home Internationals: Royal Windsor Horse Show and other invited competitions.

The DAKS Home International Mounted Games Championships, held annually at the Royal Windsor Horse Show (RWHS), is an invitational competition featuring Pony Club members from England, Scotland, Wales, Northern Ireland, and the Republic of Ireland. Dates for National Selection Trials can be found on the website and in the Fixtures section at the back of this rulebook.

District Commissioners are invited to nominate members for the National Selection Trials for RWHS and other invitational competitions.

Members must have obtained their C test before the date of nomination.

The pony ridden at the Trial must be the same one the member will ride at RWHS and any other international competition

The nominee should be a strong Mounted Games rider and an excellent representative for their Branch and country.

Members must be free from any restrictions imposed under the Transfer Rule by the nomination closing date.

Only members eligible to compete in their Area competition may attend a Selection Trial.

Nomination criteria may vary by country; please check the nomination form for specifics.

d)   International Mounted Games Exchange (IMGE)

The International Mounted Games Exchange allows Pony Club members from around the world to visit other countries, participate in competitions, and engage in cultural and social activities.

District Commissioners are invited to nominate one member for the International Mounted Games Exchange between Great Britain, Australia, Canada, and the USA.

Members must have obtained their C+ test before the date of nomination.

Members must turn 16 within the calendar year of the exchange.

The nominee should be a strong Mounted Games rider and an excellent representative for their Branch and country.

Members must be free from any restrictions imposed under the Transfer Rule by the nomination closing date.

District Commissioners must provide a confidential character reference.

District Commissioners are also required to include a copy of the Branch programmes, clearly marking the rallies and events the member has attended, and/or provide a report from PELHAM detailing the member's achievements and attendance over the past two years.

20.   GENERAL RULES

The following rules will apply in all events unless stated to the contrary in the rules for a particular event.

a)   Withdrawals (All competitions & Championships): If a Branch withdraws a Team or individual prior to the closing date for a competition, a full refund of entry and stabling fees will be made, less an administration charge. Withdrawals after the closing date for a competition will not be refunded.

b)   Abandonment (All competitions & Championships): In the event of a competition being abandoned, for whatever reason, a refund of 50% of the entry fee will be given. In such an instance the refund process will be communicated and must be followed.

c)   Tack & Turnout Inspection: It is the competitors' responsibility to ensure that their tack is in accordance with the rules and that they present themselves for inspection. Riders and ponies will be inspected before the start in the clothing and saddlery in which they are to compete, and these will not be changed thereafter without reference to the Official Steward, failure to do so may entail disqualification from the Competition. Turnout Judges will report any Riders whom they think may be over-weight for their ponies.

Any unusual decoration of the horse with unnatural things, such as ribbons, flowers, glitter etc. in the mane/tail or applied to the coat is forbidden. Red bows should be worn in the tail of ponies that kick, **Green ribbons for young horses and Yellow ribbons for registered Para riders (following**

permission from the Pony Club Office) are allowed.

d)   **Initial Parade:** At the beginning of each competition, Teams will parade in the arena, where rosettes will be awarded to the top three placed Teams in the Tack & Turnout Competition.

e)   **Objections:** Only District Commissioners or their appointed representatives, as named on the Declaration Form, are entitled to request information or lodge objections. These must be made promptly and verbal to the Official Steward.

If a District Commissioner cannot attend, they must appoint an experience substitute, preferably a senior Branch Committee member, who must also be listed on the Declaration Form. This substitute cannot be the Team trainer/manager or a competitor's parent.

No objections will be accepted regarding the starting, judging, or stewarding of any event. Other objections related to a heat or final must be made and, if possible, resolved before the next heat or final begins.

Objections concerning the equipment or arena layout must be submitted no later than half an hour before the start of the Competition. Objections regarding a rider's weight may be raised at any time during the Competition.

To minimise disruption, objections to a rider's or pony's eligibility must be made as soon as possible before the Competition begins. If a breach of eligibility is discovered later, the Mounted Games Committee may disquali the affected Team, even post-Competition.

Objections related to the result must be lodged before awards are presented.

Video evidence will not be accepted.

If the Official Steward cannot provide a decision on the day, the matter ma be referred to the Mounted Games Committee for adjudication..

21.   JUDGES AND OFFICIALS

a)   **Tack & Turnout:** Judges can be selected from the senior Officials or they can be specially appointed by the Organiser. It is recommended that the Area Representatives and someone familiar with Mounted Games Turnout are invited to judge. The Tack & Turnout Judges will attend the Initial Parade to ensure no item of tack/clothing has been changed since their inspection.

Team trainers or their nominee must accompany their Teams during the inspection.

Organisers must provide a steward for the Judges inspecting Turnout, who will make a note of any faults.

b) **Official Steward:** An Official Steward will be appointed by The Mounted Games Committee for Area Competitions, Zone Finals and National Finals. They carry out the briefing before the start of the competition. Their duties are to adjudicate any objections, to decide on eliminations and to ensure that the competition is run in accordance with the Rules. They may replace any Line Stewards if necessary.

They may, on their own initiative, "object" and take action on any matter which comes to their notice. Their decision is final.

c) **Line Judges:** Line Judges determine the order in which competitors cross the finish line but are not responsible for infringements. At Zone Finals, they will coordinate with the Official Steward regarding Start/Finish Line infringements. The Judges receive reports of eliminations from the Official Steward and, considering these, provide the results of each heat and final. They should position themselves at the same end of the finishing line as the Commentator for effective communication.

d) **Line Stewards:** Each lane at Area Competitions must have two Line Stewards, positioned at the top of the arena in line with their lanes, as outlined in APPENDIX F. Stewards at the top of the arena should stand in line with their respective lanes. If there are not enough Line Stewards available, the Official Steward may adopt the following guideline from Zone Finals:

▸   **At Zone Finals:** Line Stewards are appointed by the Mounted Games committee. They will be individuals who have no conflict of interest with any competing team. In such cases, only two- or four-Line Stewards will be positioned at the Start/Finish Line, and errors will not be boarded at the Changeover End.

e) If a Line Steward Coordinator is appointed, they will organise and supervise the rotation of stewards and report any issues to the Official Steward. For the Pairs Competition only, there may be two experienced Line Stewards at the Start Line and two at the changeover end.

f) **Starter:** The instructions for the Starter are set out in APPENDIX F.

g) **Judges' Writers (Two are advised, one for each Judge):** The Judge's Writer fills in the results of each heat and final on the Judge's Slips (obtainable by the Organiser from Wainwrights Screenprints) and takes these slips promptly to the Announcer and Scorer. These slips must be retained by the Organiser.

h) **Scorer:** The Scorer keeps the scores on the Official Sheet. A scoreboard may be displayed, but results on Pony Club Results are strongly encouraged (and compulsory for Area competitions). The Official score sheets must be sent to The Pony Club Office by the Official Steward at the end of the competition.

i) **Announcer:** The Announcer should give a short explanation of each event. They call in the Teams for each heat and final and they announce colours and positions at the start. They announce the results of heats and finals and gives aggregate scores of the Teams after each event.

j) **Collecting Ring Stewards:** They keep order in the Collecting Ring and get Teams ready to send them into the Arena when required. They should deal through the Team Trainers, who must remain in the Collecting Ring. Any difficulty in the Collecting Ring should be reported immediately to the Official Steward.

Note: Only the Team Trainer and ONE other person aged 18 years old or over may be in the collecting ring with their Team and should stand in the 'trainers track' if one is available.

k) **Arena Party:** The Arena Party puts up and issues equipment and ensures that everything is ready for each event, removing the equipment when it is no longer required.

l) **Equipment Steward:** There should be one Equipment Steward to ensure all equipment is ready before the competition starts and check that all equipment is placed correctly for each race..

22. THE COMPETITION

a) **The Start:** The signal to start will be the drop of a flag. The starter may order an unruly pony to stand behind the 6m line.

The starter alone is responsible that the start is fair, so if, after dropping their flag, they consider the start was unfair, they must immediately raise the flag again and recall the riders by whistle.

b) **Loose Ponies:** Loose ponies leaving the arena will result in elimination. If a rider deliberately releases the pony, for example, to replace equipment, the Team may be eliminated from the event at the discretion of the Official Steward. No person may enter the ring to catch a loose pony.

However, if it is safe to do so, anyone in the arena may catch a loose pony only after it has left the field of play. They may return the pony to the rider or another Team member but may not assist in any other way. The Team may then continue from the point where the infringement occurred.

c)   The result: The result of a race will be decided by the order in which the ponies' heads cross the finishing line when ridden or the riders cross the line when dismounted (as in the Sack Race). When ponies finish in Pairs, it is the head of the second pony which counts.

d)   After a race: Riders will stay in the arena when they have finished their parts in an event and must not ride down the course until all Teams have completed the event and are signalled to do so by the starter. Competitors must leave the Arena at walk.

e)   Pony Encouragement: The hand, the reins or other article must not be used as a whip.

f)   6m Box:

i.   At a changeover, the next rider to start must take up position in the 6m box. They must go next and may not be replaced by one of the others for any reason. The remainder of the Team must be behind the 6m line.

ii.   Handovers from one rider to the next must take place behind the line (i.e. the whole of the outgoing rider and his pony must be behind the line until the incoming rider and their pony have crossed it). Should the outgoing rider cross the line too soon, their Team will be eliminated unless they return to correct the error.

g)   Backing Off: Deliberate backing off behind the 6m line or indeed any other action by the next rider at a Changeover which facilitates a "flying" changeover is not permitted. The Official Steward may eliminate a Team which seeks to take this advantage.

h)   Changeovers:

i.   No rider may help another unless they are both involved in a changeover.

ii.   When correcting mistakes, only the rider(s) concerned should be in the field of play. All other riders must remain behind the line. However, should a rider/pony step accidentally into the field of play during a race, the Team will not be penalised providing the error is corrected promptly.

iii.   A Team Member may assist another by leading a pony UP TO the 6m line but may NOT lead them INTO the 6m box.

iv.   At the changeover, should the article be dropped, only the incoming rider may pick it up and hand it to the outgoing rider. They may dismount to do this or remain mounted.

i)   Retrieving articles dropped or upset:

i.   No article may be put in the mouth, on penalty of elimination.

ii.   Should a rider drop an article they have to carry, they may dismount or remain mounted to pick it up by hand, after which they must remount to resume the event from where the article was dropped.

iii.   When a rider has made a genuine attempt to put an article they are carrying into or to remove an article from a container or to place an article on or to take it off a table, pole etc and drops the article in the process, they must pick it up mounted or dismounted and if appropriate place it where it needs to go. This may be done mounted or dismounted. If dismounted they should then re- mount and continue the race.

iv.   When correcting an error, dismounted, the rider must continue to hold the pony by the rein throughout.

v.   If any equipment becomes dislodged after the incoming rider has crossed the line, then the outgoing rider must correct it and then return to start their part in the race.

j)   Correcting Errors: Should a rider knock over a container, table, post etc. while making a genuine attempt to put an article they are carrying where it needs to go, the rider must replace the knocked over equipment where it should go. This does not need to be touching the mark on the ground but needs to be in the general original position.

This may be done mounted or dismounted. The rider should then put in place the article they are carrying from either a mounted or dismounted position. If the rider has not made a genuine attempt to put the article they were carrying in the correct position, then after replacing the knocked over equipment, they must be mounted before placing the article they were carrying in the correct place. The penalty for not correcting properly is elimination from that race.

A rider who commits an error during an event may return to correct it, even after crossing the changeover or finishing line, provided the Official Steward has not declared the race to be over.

k)   Broken Equipment: Any misuse causing broken equipment will entail Elimination. The race will not be re-run.

l)   Bending – Definition: In all races in which the riders weave round bending poles the following will apply:

i.   The riders may pass the first pole on either the right or the left. Thereafter, they weave alternately to the left and right of successive poles.

ii.   MISSED POLE: Provided a rider returns and rides round the pole they do not need to continue the same bend as previously.

iii.   The following faults will incur elimination of the Team from an event.

▸   Missing a pole unless corrected.

▸   Failure by the rider concerned to replace a pole he had knocked down.

m)   Mounted Definitions: Riders must always remain mounted in the arena, except during races that require dismounting, and must exit the arena mounted. Noncompliance will result in elimination. Riders must face forward, with legs astride the saddle, and reins must always be over the pony's head. If a rider falls off and loses their pony, they must remount unaided and resume the race as close as possible to the point of dismounting.

n)   Interference: If any rider or his pony interferes with another Team during an event so as to disadvantage that other Team, the offending Team may be eliminated or in serious cases disqualified at the discretion of the Official Steward. Races will not be re-run when a Team upsets the equipment of another Team, but the offending Team will be eliminated from the race.

o)   Officials: It is forbidden for anyone other than officials to enter the arena during the competition, except the District Commissioner (or their appointed representative, if they are not able to be present) to lodge an objection. Team trainers are not allowed in the arena during the competition.

p)   Substitutions: If any pony/rider is injured before the start of a race, they may be substituted by the nominated fifth pony/rider, even if the injury occurs whilst on the start line.

q)   Race Substitutions: If for any reason an event cannot be run, it may either be replaced by the Spare Event or be declared void at the discretion of the Official Steward.

JUNIOR COMPETITION ONLY: Riders in difficulty must have made a reasonable attempt to re-mount before seeking help from a Line Steward or a fellow Team Member.

i. Juniors may lead their pony to the changeover end where the Line Steward may hold the pony whilst they remount.

ii. Juniors may lead their pony to the start/finish line where a fellow mounted Team member may hold the pony whilst they re-mount. In a Heat – Any Team receiving help to remount will score ONE Point but WILL NOT qualify for the Final.

iii. Any additional help from a steward e.g. picking up equipment, leg-up etc. will entail elimination.

iv. In a Final – Any Team receiving help to remount will score ONE Point only.

23.   COMPETITIONS – GENERAL

Notes:

1. Teams should be trained to correct their mistakes and not to play to the Line Stewards' signals. The signals are for the information of the Official Steward.

2. In the event of an obstruction by any Team, the Line Steward of the Team causing the obstruction will not signal until the end of the race.

3. The rules for all games concerning the position of equipment, or that the Number Five holding equipment, are that they must be 3m behind the Changeover line. The position will be marked by a circle.

4. In all cases of broken, dropped or upset equipment, General Rules will apply, unless stated otherwise.

5. In all Events, competitors and their ponies must cross the Start/Finish and Changeover lines between the corner markers marked with an X on the Arena Plan. This is deemed as being 'The Field of Play'.

24.   PRINCE PHILIP CUP AREA GAMES 2025

EVENT 1: Bending

Five Bending Poles are placed in a line 7 to 9 metres apart. All four riders are mounted at the Start/Finish End.

On the signal to start, Number One, carrying a Baton, rides down and back through the Bending Poles. After crossing the Start/Finish Line, they hand the Baton to Number Two. Numbers Two, Three and Four will similarly ride down and back through the Bending Poles in succession.

The winning Team will be the one whose Number Four is first over the Start/Finish Line, mounted and carrying the Baton. Any Pole which is knocked down must be replaced by the rider concerned, who must go back and resume the race from the point where the Pole was knocked down. They can resume by bending either side of the position of the Pole which was knocked down and not necessarily on the same bend as before.

If a Pole is missed, the rider can correct by returning to the missed Pole, continuing from this point on either side of the Pole.

Line Stewards will not signal unless a Pole is broken or lying flat on the ground.

EVENT 2: Hollywood Bowl Ball and Cone

There will be two cones for each team placed level with Poles 1 and 4   A tennis ball is placed on the cone level with Pole 4.   Numbers One and Three will be mounted behind the Start/Finish Line and Numbers Two and Four behind the Changeover Line.

On the signal to start Number One, carrying a tennis ball, rides to the cone level with Pole 1 and places the tennis ball on it.   They then ride to the cone level with Pole 4, collect the tennis ball and cross the Changeover Line to hand it to Number Two.   Number Two rides to the cone level with Pole 4 and places the tennis ball on it.   They then ride to the cone level with Pole 1, collect the tennis ball and cross the Start/Finish Line to hand it to Number Three. Numbers Three and Four complete the race in a similar manner.   The winning Team is the one whose Number Four is first over the Start/Finish Line carrying the tennis ball.

In the case of cones knocked over or a ball being dropped, General Rules apply.

EVENT 3: Concierge Medical Bandage and First Aid Bin (Sock & Bucket)

At the Changeover End each Team will have four bandages. They will be placed on the ground in the circle 3 metres beyond the Changeover Line. A row of buckets will be placed across the Centre Line, one for each Team.

All four riders form up behind the Start/Finish line.

On the signal to start, Number One, carrying a bandage, rides to their

Team's bucket and drops the bandage into it. They ride towards the Changeover Line, dismount, pick up a bandage, remount and return over the Start/Finish Line to hand it to Number Two.

Numbers Two, Three and Four will complete the race in the same way in succession, with Number Four dropping the last bandage into the bucket on their way back.

The winning Team will be the one whose Number Four is first over the Start/Finish Line with five bandages in their bucket.

Bandages knocked out of the circle should be replaced by the Line Steward concerned. If a bandage is knocked into the field of play and cannot be retrieved safely by the Line Steward, the rider collecting that bandage must pick it up and carry it over the Changeover Line before mounting and continuing the race.

EVENT 4: PG Sports Pyramid (Spell PGUK)

A Table will be placed on the Centre Line and another placed 3 metres behind the Changeover Line.

On the latter Table will be placed four unstacked Plastic Boxes weighing 500 grams each with a printed letter on each side. As you look from the Start/Finish Line they will be placed as follows.

'K' Front Right

'U' Back Right

'G' Back Left

'P' Front Left

On the signal to start, Number One rides to the Table behind the Changeover Line and collects the Plastic Box with the letter 'K' and rides to place it on the Table on the Centre Line. Number One then returns to cross the Start/ Finish Line.

Number Two rides to the Table behind the Changeover Line, collects the Plastic Box with the letter 'U' and stacks this upon the previous Plastic Box placed on the Table on the Centre Line. Number Two then returns to cross the Start/Finish Line.

In turn Number Three (collecting the Plastic Box with the letter 'G') and Number Four (collecting the Plastic Box with the letter 'P'), complete in a similar manner and the winning Team is the one whose Number Four is first over the Start/Finish Line with all four Plastic Boxes stacked on the Table on the Centre Line spelling from the top P G U K.

After collecting a Plastic Box, the rider may adjust the stack by hand or with the Plastic Box before or after placing their Plastic Box on the stack.

If a Table is knocked over, or a Plastic Box falls, the rider concerned may dismount to replace them. At the Changeover End this may be done in any order, but the Plastic Boxes must be placed side by side, not on top of each other.

At the Table on the Centre Line the Plastic Boxes must be stacked upright and in the correct order.

Line Stewards will only board once an incorrect Plastic Box has been placed on the Table on the Centre Line

EVENT 5: Tally Ho Farm Tack Shop

A Bending Pole topped with a Penny Dish will be erected level with Pole 1. A plastic Grooming Tray will be placed upon a Table level with Pole 4.

Number Five stands behind a Table placed 3 metres behind the Changeover Line. On this Table will be four items (a dandy brush, tin of saddle soap or shoe polish, tail bandage and a curry comb), as you look from the Start/Finish Line they will be placed as follows.

Front right – Tail Bandage

Back Right – Dandy Brush

Back Left – Rubber Curry Comb

Front Left - Tin of Saddle Soap or Shoe Polish.

Number One will carry a Coin (10cm diameter). On the signal to start Number One rides and places the Coin in the Penny Dish, continues to collect the Grooming Tray and then rides to Number Five who puts any one of the items in the Grooming Tray. Number One then returns the Grooming Tray onto the Table level with Pole 4. They then ride to the Penny Dish, collect the Coin and hand it to Number Two behind the Start/Finish Line. Numbers Two, Three and Four will complete the race in the same way.

The winning Team will be the one whose Number Four is first over the Start/Finish Line carrying the Coin with all four items in the Grooming Tray on the Table level with pole 4.

If an item is dropped behind the Changeover Line, either the rider or Number Five may pick it up. The item must be in the Grooming Tray before the rider re-crosses the Changeover Line. Number Five may hold the rein of the pony behind the Changeover Line.

Number Five must remain behind the Table at the changeover end. They can move to retrieve a piece of dropped equipment but must return to their position behind the Table before continuing their role in the race.

EVENT 6: Tyre

A motorcycle Tyre will be placed on the Centre Line for each Team.

Numbers One and Two will form up behind the Start/Finish Line, with Number Four behind the 6 metre Line. Number Three will be behind the Changeover Line.

On the signal to start, Numbers One and Two ride to the Tyre where Number One dismounts, hands their pony to Number Two, gets through the Tyre and remounts. Both riders then continue across the Changeover Line where Number One will wait.

Numbers Two and Three then ride to the Tyre where Number Two dismounts, hands their pony to Number Three, gets through the Tyre and remounts. Both riders then continue across the Start/Finish Line and Number Two leaves the race.

Numbers Three and Four then ride to the Tyre where Number Three dismounts, hands their pony to Number Four, gets through the Tyre and remounts. Both riders then continue across the Changeover Line. Number Three drops out and Number Four and Number One complete the race in a similar way with Number Four going through the Tyre.

The winning Team will be the one whose final pair (Numbers One and Four) cross the Start/Finish Line first, mounted on their ponies.

At each changeover, the next pony to go must remain behind the Line until both incoming riders have crossed it.

The rider who is to lead the pony may take hold of the rein behind the Line or as they go down the arena. The pony must be led by the rein nearer the ridden pony and not by the bit ring or any other part of the bridle. The Tyre may not be touched until the pony has been correctly handed over. Riders may not run with the Tyre.

The Tyre must remain between Poles 2 and 3 and in the Team's lane throughout the race. If the Tyre rolls or is dragged outside of Poles 2 and 3 i their lane, then the dismounted rider must retrieve it before resuming the race.

EVENT 7: EGUK 2 Mug

Four Bending Poles are placed in a line 7 to 9 metres apart. Mugs are placed on Poles 1 and 3.

Numbers One and Three are mounted at the Start/Finish End, Numbers Two and Four at the Changeover End.

On the signal to start Number One rides down the arena, moves the Mug from Pole 1 to Pole 2,then the Mug from Pole 3 to Pole 4 and then rides across the Changeover Line.

Number Two rides down the arena, moves the Mug from Pole 4 to Pole 3, then the Mug from Pole 2 to Pole 1 and then crosses the Start/Finish Line. Number Three repeats the actions of Number One and Number Four repeats the actions of Number Two.

The winning Team is the one whose Number Four crosses the Start/Finish Line first with Mugs on Poles 1 and 3.

Mugs must be placed on each Pole in the correct order, should one fall or is missed the rider must replace the mug before continuing, if the next Mug has already been moved then the rider must replace this Mug on the correct pole before correcting the first error.

EVENT 8: 4 Flag

There will be three Flag Cones for each team, one placed level with Pole 1, one on the Centre Line and one level with Pole 5. Four Flags will be placed in the Flag Cone on the Centre Line.

All four riders are mounted at the Start/Finish End.

On the signal to start Number One rides to the Flag Cone on the Centre Line, picks up a flag, and rides to place the Flag into either the Flag Cone level with Pole 1 or the Flag Cone level with Pole 5. The rider then proceeds to cross the Start/Finish Line.

Numbers Two, Three and Four repeat the actions of Number One by collecting a Flag from the Flag Cone on the Centre Line and placing it in one of the other Flag Cones. The order in which Flags are placed into Flag Cones is not determined by these rules. The winning team is the one whose Number Four is first over the Start/Finish Line with two Flags in each of the Flag Cones level with Poles 1 and 5, leaving the Flag Cone on the Centre Line empty.

Flag Cones knocked over must be set up immediately by the rider concerned.   Should a flag come off the cane, the cane alone may be used. On windy days rubber bands may be used to keep the Flags furled.

SPARE: 2 Flag

There will be two Flag Cones for each Team, placed level with Poles 1 and 4. A Flag will be placed in the Flag Cone level with Pole 4.

Numbers One and Three will be at the Start/Finish End with Numbers Two and Four at the Changeover End.

On the signal to start, Number One, carrying a Flag, rides to the Flag Cone level with Pole 1 and places the Flag in it. They then ride to the Flag Cone level with Pole 4, take out the Flag and hand it to Number Two behind the Changeover Line.

Number Two rides to the Flag Cone level with Pole 4 and places the Flag in it. They then ride to the Flag Cone level with Pole 1, take out the Flag and hand it to Number Three behind the Start/Finish Line.

Numbers Three and Four will repeat the actions of Numbers One and Two respectively.

Flag Cones knocked over must be set up immediately by the rider concerned.

Should a flag come off the cane, the cane alone may be used to complete the race.

The winning Team is the one whose Number Four is first over the Start/ Finish Line carrying a Flag

25.   JUNIOR AREA GAMES 2025

EVENT 1: Hollywood Bowl Bending

The details of this game are set out in Prince Philip Cup (Senior) Area Games, Event Number One.

EVENT 2: Concierge Medical Bandage and First Aid Bin (Sock & Bucket) (Junior Version)

A Bending Pole topped with a Penny Dish containing four bandages will be placed 3 metres behind the Changeover Line. On the Centre Line there wi be a row of buckets, one for each Team.

All four riders form up at the Start/Finish End.

On the signal to start, Number One, carrying a bandage rides to their Team's bucket and drops the bandage into it. They then continue over the Changeover Line, collect a bandage from the Penny Dish and return across the Start/Finish Line to hand it to Number Two.

Numbers Two, Three and Four will complete the race in the same way in succession, with Number Four dropping the last bandage into the bucket on their way back.

If a bandage or bandages are knocked out of the Penny Dish they must be replaced by the rider concerned.

The winning Team will be the one whose Number Four is first over the Start/ Finish Line with five bandages in their bucket

EVENT 3: Tally Ho Farm Tack Shop

The details of this game are set out in Prince Philip Cup (Senior) Area Games, Event number 5.

EVENT 4: Tyre

The details of this game are set out in Prince Philip Cup (Senior) Area Games, Event number 6.

EVENT 5: PGUK Pyramid (Junior Version)

A Table will be placed on the Centre Line and another placed 3 metres behind the Changeover Line. Number Five will be standing behind the Table behind the Changeover Line and must not encroach down either side of the Table.

On the latter Table will be placed four unstacked Plastic Boxes weighing 500 grams each with a printed letter on each side. As you look from the Start/ Finish Line they will be placed as follows.

'K' Front right

'U' Back Right

'G' Back Left

'P' Front Left

On the signal to start, Number One rides across the Changeover Line and collects from Number Five the Plastic Box with the letter 'K' and places it on the Table on the Centre Line. Number One then returns to cross the Start/Finish Line.

Number Two rides to the Changeover Line, collects the Plastic Box with the letter 'U' from Number Five and stacks this upon the previous Plastic Box placed on the Table on the Centre Line. Number Two then returns to cross the Start/Finish Line.

In turn Numbers Three and Four, collecting respectively the Plastic Boxes with letters "G" and "P" on them, complete in a similar manner and the winning team is the one whose Number Four is first over the Start/Finish Line with all four Plastic Boxes stacked on the Table on the Centre Line spelling from the top P G U K.

After being given a Plastic Box, the rider may adjust the stack by hand or with the Plastic Box before or after placing their Plastic Box on the stack.

If the Table on the Centre Line is knocked over, or a Plastic Box falls, the rider concerned may dismount to replace them. The Plastic Boxes must be stacked upright and in the correct order.

If the Table behind the Changeover Line is knocked over, or a Plastic Box is knocked off this Table or is dropped by Number Five, they may collect the Plastic Box but must (if necessary) replace the Table on its correct location and stand behind it before handing the Plastic Box over to the rider.

If a Plastic Box is knocked off the Table at the Changeover Line by Number Five whilst the rider is in the field of play, then that rider must return over the Changeover Line and either wait until the Plastic Box is replaced or, if it already has been replaced, cross the line and continue with the race. If the rider has already placed their Plastic Box on the Table on the Centre Line, they must pick this Plastic Box up and return over the Changeover Line and wait for the Plastic Box which has been knocked off to be replaced before continuing with the race. Plastic Boxes must be placed side by side but not on top of each other.

Line Stewards will only board once the incorrect Plastic Box has been placed on the Centre Line Table.

EVENT 6: EGUK 2 Mug

The details of this game are set out in Prince Philip Cup (Senior) Area Games, Event number 7.

EVENT 7: 4 Flag

The details of this game are set out in Prince Philip Cup (Senior) Area Games, Event number 8.

SPARE: 2 Flag

The details of this game are set out in Prince Philip Cup (Senior) Area Games, Spare Event.

26.   PAIRS AREA GAMES 2025

EVENT 1: Bending (Pairs)

Five Bending Poles are placed in a line 7 to 9 metres apart. Both riders are mounted at the Start/Finish End.

On the signal to start, Number One, carrying a Baton, rides down and back through the Bending Poles. After crossing the Start/Finish Line they hand the Baton to Number Two. Number Two will similarly ride down and back through the Bending Poles.

The winning Pair will be the one whose Number Two crosses the Start/Finish Line first, mounted, carrying the Baton.

Any Bending Pole which is knocked down must be replaced by the rider concerned; they must then go back and resume the race from the point where the Bending Pole was knocked down. They may resume by bending either side of the position of the Bending Pole which was knocked down and not necessarily on the same bend as before.

If a Pole is missed, the rider can correct by returning to the missed Pole, continuing from this point on either side of the Pole.

Line Stewards will not signal unless the Bending Pole is broken or lying flat on the ground.

EVENT 2: Hollywood Bowl Ball and Cone (Pairs)

There will be two cones for each Pair placed level with Poles 1 and 4.   A tennis ball is placed on the cone level with Pole 4. Number One will be mounted behind the Start/Finish Line and Number Two behind the Changeover Line.

On the signal to start Number One, carrying a tennis ball, rides to the cone level with Pole 1, places their ball on it, rides to the cone level with Pole 4, collects the tennis ball and hands it to Number Two behind the Changeover

Line.   Number Two rides to the cone level with Pole 4, places their ball on it rides to the cone level with Pole 1, collects the tennis ball and rides to cross the Start/Finish Line.   The winning Pair is the one whose Number Two is first over the Start/Finish line carrying a tennis ball.

In the case of cones knocked over or a tennis ball being dropped, General Rules apply.

EVENT 3: Concierge Medical Bandage and First Aid Bin (Sock & Bucket) (Pairs)

At the Changeover End each Pair will have two bandages, placed on the ground in the circle 3 metres beyond the Changeover Line. Across the Centre Line will be a row of buckets, one for each pair.

Both riders form up behind the Start/Finish Line

On the signal to start, Number One, carrying a bandage, rides to their Pair's bucket and drops the bandage into it. They then ride towards the Changeover Line, dismount, pick up a bandage, remount and return across the Start/Finish Line to hand it to Number Two.

Number Two will complete the race in the same way but with Number Two dropping the last bandage into the bucket on their way back.

The winning Pair will be the one whose Number Two is first over the Start/Finish Line with three bandages in the bucket.

Bandages knocked out of the circle should be replaced by the Line Steward concerned. If a bandage is knocked into the field of play and cannot be retrieved safely by the Line Steward, the rider collecting that bandage must pick it up and carry it over the Changeover Line before mounting and continuing the race.

EVENT 4: PG Sports Pyramid (Spell PGUK) (Pairs)

A Table will be placed on the Centre Line and another 3 metres behind the Changeover Line.

On the latter Table will be placed four unstacked Plastic Boxes - each with a printed letter on each side. As you look from the Start/Finish Line they will be placed as follows.

'K' Front right

'U' Back Right

'G' Back Left

'P' Front Left

At the signal to start, Number One rides to the Table behind the Changeover Line and collects the Plastic Box with the letter 'K' and rides to place it on the Table on the Centre Line. Number One then returns to the Table behind the Changeover Line and collects the letter 'U' and rides to place this on the previous Plastic Box placed on the Table on the Centre Line and then crosses the Start/Finish Line.

Number Two rides to the Table behind the Changeover Line and, in a similar manner to Number One, collects the Plastic Box with the letter 'G' followed by one with the letter 'P' and places each of them upon the stack of Plastic Boxes on the Table on the Centre Line.

After collecting a Plastic Box, the rider may adjust the stack by hand or with the Plastic Box before or after placing their Plastic Box on the stack.

If a Table is knocked over, or a Plastic Box falls, the rider concerned may dismount to replace them. At the Changeover End this may be done in any order, but the Plastic Boxes must be placed side by side, not on top of each other.

At the Table on the Centre Line the Plastic Boxes must be stacked upright and in the correct order.

The winning Pair is the one whose Number Two is first over the Start/Finish Line with all four Plastic Boxes stacked on the Table on the Centre Line spelling from the top P G U K.

Line Stewards will only board once the incorrect Plastic Box has been placed on the Table on the Centre Line.

EVENT 5: Tally Ho Farm Tack Shop (Pairs)

A Bending Pole topped with a Penny Dish will be erected level with Pole 1. A plastic Grooming Tray will be placed upon a Table level with Pole 4. A second Table will be placed 3 metres behind the Changeover Line. On this Table will be four items (a dandy brush, tin saddle soap or shoe polish, tail bandage and a curry comb) as you look from the Start/Finish Line they will be placed as follows.

Front right – Tail Bandage

Back Right – Dandy Brush

Back Left – Rubber Curry Comb

Front Left - Tin of Saddle Soap or Shoe Polish

Number One will carry a Coin (10cm diameter). On the signal to start Number One rides and places the Coin in the Penny Dish. Number One then rides across the Changeover Line and collects from the Table any one item, places the item in the Grooming Tray, rides back over the Changeover Line, collects a second item from the Table and places it in the Grooming Tray. They then ride to the Penny Dish collect the Coin and hand it to Number Two behind the Start/Finish Line. Number Two completes the race in the same way.

If a Table is knocked over, or an item falls, the rider concerned may dismount to replace them.

The winning Pair will be the one whose Number Two is first over the Start/Finish Line carrying the Coin with all four items in the Grooming Tray on the Table level with Pole 4.

EVENT 6: Tyre (Pairs)

A motorcycle Tyre will be placed on the Centre Line. Each pair will form up behind the Start/Finish Line.

On the signal to start, Number One and Two will ride to the Tyre where Number One dismounts, hands their pony to Number Two, gets through the Tyre and remounts. Both riders then continue to cross the Changeover Line where the Pair will turn and ride back towards the Tyre. Number Two dismounts, hands their pony to Number One, gets through the Tyre and remounts. The Pair then rides over the Start/Finish Line.

The winning Pair will be the one which crosses the Start/Finish Line first, mounted on their ponies.

The rider who is to lead the pony may take hold of the rein behind the line or as they go down the arena. The pony must be led by the rein nearer the ridden pony and not by the bit ring or any part of the bridle. The Tyre may not be touched until the pony has been correctly handed over. Riders are not allowed to run with the Tyre.

The Tyre must remain between Poles 2 and 3 and in the Pair's lane throughout the race. If the Tyre rolls or is dragged outside of Poles 2 and 3 the Pair's lane, then the dismounted rider must retrieve it before resuming the race.

EVENT 7: EGUK 2 Mug (Pairs)

Four Bending Poles are placed in a line 7 to 9 metres apart. Mugs are placed on Poles 1 and 3.

Number One is mounted behind the Start/Finish Line and Number Two is mounted behind the Changeover Line.

On the signal to start Number One rides down the arena, moves the Mug from Pole 1 to Pole 2, then Mug from Pole 3 to Pole 4 and then rides across the Changeover Line.

Number Two rides down the arena, moves the Mug from Pole 4 to Pole 3, then the Mug from Pole 2 to Pole 1 and then crosses the Start/Finish Line.

The winning Pair is the one whose Number Two crosses the Start/Finish Line first with Mugs on Poles 1 and 3.

Mugs must be placed on each Pole in the correct order. Should one fall or is missed the rider must replace the Mug before continuing. If the next Mug has already been moved, then the rider must replace this Mug on the correct pole before correcting the first error.

EVENT 8: 4 Flag (Pairs)

There will be three Flag Holders for each Pair, one placed level with Pole 1, one on the Centre Line, and one level with Pole 5. Four flags will be placed in the Flag Cone on the Centre Line

On the signal to start Number One rides to the Flag Cone on the Centre Line, picks up a Flag, rides to either of the other Flag Cones and places the Flag in it. They then return to the Flag Cone on the Centre Line, pick up another Flag and place the Flag in either of the other Flag Cones. They then ride back to cross the Start/Finish line.

The Number Two rides to the Flag Cone on the Centre Line, picks up a Flag, rides to either of the other Flag Cones and places the Flag in it. They then return to the Flag Cone on the Centre Line pick up the final Flag and place it in either of the other Flag Cones and then ride back to cross the Start/Finish Line.

The winning Pair is the one whose Number Two is first over the Start/Finish Line with two Flags in each of the Flag Cones level with Poles 1 and 5, leaving the Flag Cone on the Centre Line empty. Flag Cones knocked over must be set up immediately by the rider concerned.

Should a Flag come off the cane, the cane alone may be used. On windy days rubber bands may be used to keep the Flag furled.

SPARE: 2 Flag (Pairs)

There will be two Flag Cones for each Pair, placed level with Poles 1 and 4. A Flag will be placed in the Flag Cone level with Pole 4.

Number One, carrying a Flag, is mounted behind the Start/Finish Line and Number Two mounted behind the Changeover Line.

On the signal to start, Number One, carrying a Flag, rides to the Flag Cone level with Pole 1 and places the Flag in it. They then ride to the Flag Cone level with Pole 4, take out the Flag and hand it to Number Two behind the Changeover Line.

Number Two rides to the Flag Cone level with Pole 4 and places the Flag in it. They then ride to the Flag Cone level with Pole 1, take out the Flag and ride across the Start/Finish Line.

Flag Cones knocked over must be set up immediately by the rider concerned. Should a flag come off the cane, the cane alone may be used to complete the race.

The winning Pair is the one whose Number Two is first over the Start/Finish Line carrying a Flag.

27.   PRINCE PHILIP CUP ZONE GAMES 2025

EVENT 1: Concierge Medical Post Box (Race requires 5 members)

A Bending Pole topped with a Penny Dish will be set up level with Pole 1.

On the Centre Line will be a Post Box with its feet astride the Centre Line.

Number Five will stand with four Brochures in the circle 3 metres behind the Changeover Line.

All four riders are mounted at Start/Finish End.

On the signal to start Number One, carrying a Coin (10cm in diameter), will ride to place the Coin in the Penny Dish. They then ride across the Changeover Line, collect a Brochure from Number Five, ride back to the Post Box and post the Brochure through so that it drops on the ground on the Start/Finish side of the Post Box. This must be done by pushing the Brochure through from the side of the Post Box nearer the Changeover Lin and not by pulling from the other side. They then ride to collect the Coin from the Penny Dish and hand it to Number Two behind the Start/Finish Line.

Numbers Two, Three and Four complete the race in the same way. The winning Team will be the one whose Number Four is first over the Start/Finish Line carrying the Coin.

If the Post Box is knocked over, the rider concerned must replace it. If the Post Box is knocked from its original position, providing the Post Box feet are astride the Centre Line (as per original start position), or at least one foot is touching the Centre Line the rider may continue. The Brochure must not be folded at any time during the race. The rider must make a genuine attempt to post the Brochure while mounted but provided they have done so, if they drop the Brochure they may dismount and post it unmounted

Equipment information – At Zone and Championships, the following size Post Box will be used.

Height – 122cm (to slot 94 cm)

Width - 41cm

Slot opening - 3cm x 25cm

Brochure - A4 brochures, 1cm thick, in plastic sleeve or wallet.

EVENT 2: Tennis Ball Shuffle

A pole topped with a "socket" containing a tennis ball placed in the 9 O'clock position as viewed from the Start/Finish Line is placed on the Centre Line. Ball cones are placed level with Poles 1 and 4.

Numbers One and Three are mounted at the Start/Finish End and Numbers Two and Four at the Changeover End.

On the signal to start Number One, carrying a tennis ball, rides to and places the tennis ball on the cone level with Pole 1. They then ride to the "socket", remove the tennis ball, ride to and place the tennis ball on the cone level with Pole 4 before crossing the Changeover Line.

Number Two rides to the cone level with Pole 4 collects the tennis ball and places this in the "socket" at any position. They then ride to the cone level with Pole 1, remove the tennis ball and hand it to Number Three behind the Start/Finish Line.

Number Three repeats the actions of Number One. Number Four repeats the actions of Number Two and carries the final tennis ball across the Start/Finish Line.

EVENT 3: Hollywood Bowl Bowling

Four full-sized Bottles weighted with 500 grams of sand will be placed in a line 30 centimetres apart 3 metres beyond the Changeover Line.

A Bucket with 12 weighted, plastic "Boules" will be placed in front of the Changeover Line.

All four riders are unmounted at the Start/Finish End with two ponies Numbers One and Two with one pony will form up, on foot, behind the Start/Finish Line, each facing forward and on the near side of the pony. On the signal to start, Number One mounts the pony. This must be done befor crossing the Start/Finish Line. Number Two then leads the pony across the Centre Line. Number One dismounts after the Centre Line and Number Tw waits holding the pony.

Whilst Number Two holds the pony, Number One runs to the Bucket and from behind the Changeover Line bowls/throws a Boule at the Bottles to knock down one Bottle. If they knock down more than one Bottle, Number One must reset any others upright. Number One runs to the pony and whilst Number One holds the pony, Number Two runs to the Bucket and from behind the Changeover Line bowls/throws a Boule to knock down another Bottle. If they knock down more than the one Bottle, Number Two must reset any others upright. Number Two then runs back to the pony an mounts and Number One leads and runs with the pony leading on either side of the pony. Number Two must be mounted before crossing the Centr Line. The riders then ride/run back over the Start/ Finish Line.

Riders Numbers Three and Four repeat the actions of Numbers One and Two. The winning Team is the one whose Number Four riding and Number Three leading are first over the Start/Finish Line.

If a Team completely runs out of Boules, the rider concerned must run forward with the Bucket to collect any number and then continue the race from behind the Changeover Line as before. A rider may leave an empty bucket if they have completed their part of the race.

Ponies must be led by the nearer rein throughout. If contact is lost, leader and pony must return to the point that the contact was lost before continuing. The white hat band is worn by the Number Four rider who is on the pony when crossing the Start/Finish Line.

When bowling/throwing the Boules, the rider's foot must not be touching the Changeover Line. Line Stewards will move forward and level with the Changeover Line and call 'Fault, throw again' if the rider's foot touches the line while throwing/bowling the boule. If they knock down a Bottle with their foot touching the line, they must replace the Bottle upright before throwing/bowling again.

EVENT 4: Tally Ho Farm Tack Shop (Race requires 5 members)

The details of this game are set out in Prince Philip Cup (Senior) Area Games, Event number 5.

EVENT 5: Rope

Lines of four Bending Poles will be erected approximately 7 to 9 metres apart.

Numbers One and Three will be mounted at the Start/Finish End and Numbers Two and Four at the Changeover End. Number One will carry a rope about 90 centimetres in length. The rope must not be looped or knotted throughout the race. Holding of hands during the race is not permitted.

On the signal to start, Number One will ride up weaving through the Bending Poles to cross the Changeover Line, where Number Two will grasp the rope and both riders return through the Bending Poles holding the rope to the Start/Finish Line. After crossing the Start/Finish Line, Number One will release the rope and Number Three will grasp it. Numbers Two and Three, each holding the rope, then ride up through the Bending Poles to cross the Changeover Line, where Number Two will release the rope and Number Four will grasp it. Numbers Three and Four then ride back through the Bending Poles and over the Start/Finish Line each holding the rope.

The winning team will be the one whose Numbers Three and Four cross the Start/Finish Line first, mounted and carrying the rope between them.

Each time the rope is released and passed to another rider all ponies' legs must be over the Start/Finish Line or Changeover Lines as appropriate.

Should either rider let go of the rope, they must go back and resume the race from the point where the fault occurred.

EVENT 6: Spell STRUK Pole

A Bending Pole will be set up level with Pole 1 in line with a circle at the Changeover End.

In the circle on the ground 3 metres beyond the Changeover Line will be placed randomly SEVEN Cartons. The Cartons will have the following letters S-T-R-U-K-Blank-Blank.

All four riders are mounted at the Start/Finish End.

On the signal to start Number One, carrying a Blank Carton with no letter on it rides to the Bending Pole and slots the Carton over the pole. They then continue to the Changeover End, dismount and collects a Blank Carton, remount, ride down the arena and slots this Carton over the pole and then rides back to the Changeover End, dismounts and collects another Blank Carton, remount, ride down the arena and hand the Carton to Number Two behind the Start/Finish Line.

Number Two rides to the Bending Pole and slots the Blank Carton over the pole. They then continue to the Changeover End, dismount and collect the Carton with the letter K, remount, ride down the arena and slots this Carton over the pole and then rides back to the Changeover End, dismounts and collects the Carton with the letter U, remount, ride down the arena and hand the Carton to Number Three behind the Start/Finish Line.

Number Three rides to the Bending Pole and slots the Carton (letter U) over the pole. They then continue to the Changeover End, dismount and collect the Carton with the letter R, remount, ride down the arena and slots this Carton over the pole and then rides back to the Changeover End, dismount and collects the Carton with the letter T, remount, ride down the arena and hand the Carton to Number Four behind the Start/Finish Line.

Number Four rides to the Bending Pole and slots the Carton (letter T) over the pole. They then continue to the Changeover End, dismount and collect the Carton with the letter S, remount, ride down the arena and slot the Carton (letter S) over the pole and cross the Start/Finish Line.

The winning team is the one whose Number Four is first over the Start/Finish Line and with all Cartons on the pole reading from top to bottom S, R, U, K, Blank, Blank, Blank.

Cartons placed in the wrong order, or the wrong way up, must be corrected by the rider concerned, the narrow neck of each Carton is deemed as being the top.

Cartons kicked out of the circle by a pony should be replaced by the Line Steward concerned. If a Carton is knocked into the field of play and cannot be retrieved safely by the Line Steward, the rider collecting that Carton must pick it up and carry it over the Changeover Line before mounting and continuing the race.

EVENT 7: 3-Legged Sack

Numbers One and Three will be mounted at the Start/Finish End and

Numbers Two and Four will be mounted at the Changeover End.

On the signal to start Number One carrying a sack rides up the arena, over the Changeover Line and dismounts. Number Two dismounts when Number One has crossed the Changeover Line.

Numbers One and Two each put one leg into the sack. Holding the sack in one hand and leading their ponies with the other, they run back together over the Start/Finish line.

The sack is then handed to Number Three who repeats the actions of Number One, and Number Four will repeat the actions of Number Two.

The winning team is the one whose Numbers Three and Four are first over the Start/Finish line.

The sack may be handed to the outgoing rider before the incoming rider has dismounted providing the incoming pony's feet have fully crossed the line. Ponies must be led by the nearer rein until the rider has completed their element of the race.

EVENT 8: Sword

A line of four Bending Poles will be erected approximately 7 to 9 metres apart for each team. A plastic Sword ring with a 10cm diameter hole will be placed on each of the four poles secured with an elastic band. On Poles 1 and 2 the stem of the rings by which the ring is secured will be on the back edge of the pole and on Poles 3 and 4 it will be on the front edge of the pole.

Numbers One and Three will be mounted behind the Start/Finish Line and Numbers Two and Four will be mounted behind the Changeover Line.

On the signal to start Number One holding a Sword rides up the arena, collects a ring from the top of any pole using the Sword, rides over the Changeover Line and passes the Sword with the ring still on it to Number Two. Number Two rides down the arena, collects a ring from the top of any pole using the Sword, rides over the Start/Finish Line and passes the Sword with the rings still on to Number Three. Number Three repeats the actions of Number One and Number Four repeats the actions on Number Two.

The winning Team is the one whose Number Four crosses the Start/Finish Line first holding the Sword with all four rings on it.

The Sword must be held behind the cross bar on the Sword and no part of the hand/finger shall be in front of the cross bar throughout the race.

Should a ring be knocked off a pole, or should a ring be dropped, the rider may dismount and pick it up by hand and may hold any part of the Sword. They may hold any rings on the Sword with their fingers to help collect any other rings and must go back to where the error took place and continue the race holding the Sword behind the cross bar. To help with remounting the rider may place the Sword against a pole and pick up the Sword by the blade when mounted but must go back to where the error took place and continue the race holding the Sword behind the cross bar.

If during a handover the Sword or rings are dropped, providing a genuine attempt has been made to handover then the incoming rider may dismount and collect the Sword and/or rings and still being dismounted may hand the Sword to the next outgoing rider providing they hand over the Sword with their hand behind the cross bar.

If the Sword or rings are dropped over the Changeover Line and no genuine attempt has been made to handover the Sword to the next outgoing rider, then the incoming rider can dismount and pick up the dropped Sword and/or rings but must remount before handing over the Sword to the next outgoing rider and must do so with their hand behind the cross bar.

If during a Changeover the rings are dropped into the field of play by the outgoing rider, they must correct the error and re-cross the Changeover Line before continuing with the race.

There is no penalty should a pole be knocked down.

EVENT 9: PG Sports Rosette Row (Race requires 5 members)

A litter bin containing four coloured Rosettes (each one has a large letter in the of it) with rings will be placed on the Centre Line there is. The Rosettes will be placed in a square formation:

Blue (letter P) at 12 o'clock

Red (letter G) at 3 o'clock

Green (U) at 6 o'clock

Yellow (K) at 9 o'clock

Number Five stands 3 metres behind the Changeover Line facing towards the Start/Finish Line, holding a Gibbet with the hooks facing sideways and open to Number Five's right.

All four riders form up mounted at the Start/Finish End. Number One has a cane with a small hook on one end.

On the signal to start. Number One rides to the litter bin, hooks ANY Rosette and continues over the Changeover Line to Number Five. Number Five unhooks the Rosette and secures it on the hook on the Gibbet in the correct order which will look to Number Five from left to the right: Yellow letter K, Green letter U, Red letter G, Blue letter P.

From the Start/Finish Line looking up the arena it will spell from left to right: Blue 'P', Red 'G', Green 'U', Yellow 'K' - P G U K

Number One must remain behind the Changeover Line until Number Five has correctly placed the Rosette on the hook; they then return over the Start/ Finish Line and hand the cane to Number Two. Numbers Two, Three and Four complete the race in the same way.

If a Rosette is placed on the wrong hook, this can be corrected if the rider must remain or come back over the Changeover Line while Number Five corrects it. Should the Number Five knock off a Rosette after the changeover has been completed and the rider has crossed the Changeover Line back into the field of play, the Number Five may replace the dropped Rosette on to the Gibbet without the rider needing to recross the Changeover Line.

The winning Team is the one whose Number Four is first across the Start/ Finish Line with all four Rosettes on the Gibbet in the correct order.

Should a rider drop a Rosette, they may pick it up either mounted or dismounted, before replacing it on the hook of the cane. If a Rosette is dropped whilst handing over to Number Five, the Number Five may pick it up and put it on the Gibbet (See General Rules).

The Rosette should be always on the hook when riding up the arena. If the Rosette is dropped, then the rider must pick it up and continue with the race. The cane will also have a rubber stopper 10 centimetres from the hook for safety reasons to stop the Rosette from travelling up the cane and hitting the rider's fingers. Should the Rosette go up the cane then the rider must stop and get the Rosette back onto the hook before proceeding.

EVENT 10: EGUK 5 Flag

A Flag Cone will be placed 3 metres behind the Changeover Line and another on the Centre Line. Each team will have five Flags on canes. Four of these will be in the Flag Cone on the Centre Line and one will be carried by Number One at the start.

On the signal to start Number One rides to the other end of the arena, places the Flag they are carrying in the Flag Cone behind the Changeover Line, rides back, collects a Flag out of their team's Flag Cone on the Centre

Line and hands this Flag to Number Two behind the Start/Finish Line.

Numbers Two, Three and Four will complete the race in the same way in succession so that, at the end of the race, the team will have placed four Flags in the Flag Cone behind the Changeover Line and Number Four has crossed the Start/Finish Line mounted and carrying the fifth Flag.

Should a Flag Cone be knocked over, the rider must put it up again, replacing any Flags there may have been in it. Should a rider take more than one Flag from the Flag Cone, they must replace the surplus. They may dismount to correct mistakes.

The winning team is the one whose Number Four is first over the Start/Finish Line carrying a Flag.

If the flag should come off the cane, the cane may be used to complete the race.

On windy days rubber bands can be used to keep the flags furled and prevent them blowing together.

SPARE: 2 Mug

The details of this game are set out in Prince Philip Cup (Senior) Area Games, Event number 7.

28.   JUNIOR ZONE GAMES 2025

EVENT 1: Hollywood Bowl Bending

The details of this game are set out in Prince Philip Cup (Senior) Area Games, Event number 1.

EVENT 2: Concierge Medical Bandage and First Aid Bin (Sock & Bucket)

The details of this game are set out in Prince Philip Cup (Senior) Area Games, Event number 3.

EVENT 3: PG Sports Rosette Row (Junior Version) (Race requires 5 members)

A Table will be placed on the Centre Line. On the Table will be four coloured Rosettes (each with a large letter in the centre of it) with rings on. Each Rosette is placed individually on the top of each other in the following order

1st - Blue Rosette (letter P) is placed up and down with the ring at 6 o'clock (slightly off set).

2nd - Red Rosette (letter G) is placed side to side with the ring at 9 o'clock (slightly off set).

3rd - Green Rosette (letter U) is placed up and down with the ring at 6 o'clock

4th - Yellow Rosette (letter K) is placed side to side with the ring at 9 o'clock.

Number Five stands 3 metres behind the Changeover Line towards the Star/Finish Line, holding a Gibbet with hooks facing sideways and open to Number Five's right.

All four riders form up at the Start/Finish End.

On the signal to start, Number One rides to the Table and picks up one Rosette and continues over the Changeover Line and hands the Rosette to Number Five. Number Five secures it on the correct hook on the Gibbet which will look to Number Five from left to right:

Yellow letter K, Green letter U, Red letter G, Blue letter P

From the Start/Finish Line looking up the arena it will spell from left to right: Blue 'P', Red' G', Green 'U', Yellow 'K' - P G U K

Number One must remain behind the Changeover Line until Number Five has placed the Rosette on the correct hook, they then return down the arena and over the Start/Finish Line.

Numbers Two, Three and Four each in turn complete the race in the same way.

The winning Team is the one whose Number Four is first across the Start/Finish Line with all four Rosettes on the Gibbet in the correct order.

If the Rosette is placed on the wrong hook, this can be corrected if the rider comes back over the Changeover Line while Number Five corrects it. Should the Number Five knock off a Rosette after the changeover has been completed and the rider has crossed the line back into the field of play, Number Five may replace the dropped Rosette on to the Gibbet without the rider needing to recross the Changeover Line.

Should a rider drop a Rosette, they may dismount and pick it up before continuing. If a Rosette is dropped whilst handing over to Number Five, the Number Five may pick it up and put it on the Gibbet (See General Rules). Should a rider knock off any Rosettes from the Table at the Centre Line, these can be replaced in any order.

EVENT 4: Tyre

The details of this game are set out in Prince Philip Cup (Senior) Area Games, Event number 6.

EVENT 5: Tally Ho Farm Tack Shop (Race requires 5 members)

The details of this game are set out in Prince Philip Cup (Senior) Area Games, Event number 5.

EVENT 6: Hollywood Bowl Bowling (Junior Version)

Four full-sized Bottles weighted with 500 grams of sand will be placed in a line 30 centimetres apart 2 metres beyond the Changeover Line. A Bucket with 12 weighted, plastic "Boules" will be placed in front of the Changeover Line.

Two riders are mounted with two riders unmounted at the Start/Finish End with two ponies only. Number One will be mounted behind the Start/Finish Line with Number Two standing on the near side of their pony holding the near side rein in their right hand. Numbers Three and Four will be behind the 6 metre Line similarly mounted and unmounted.

On the signal to start, Numbers One and Two ride/run over the Start/Finish Line and across the Centre Line. Number One dismounts and Number Two waits holding the pony.

Whilst Number Two holds the pony, Number One runs to the Bucket and from behind the Changeover Line bowls/throws a Boule at the Bottles to knock down only one Bottle. If they knock down more than the one Bottle Number One must reset any others upright. Number One runs to the pony and whilst Number One holds the pony, Number Two runs to the Bucket and from behind the Changeover Line bowls/throws a Boule to knock down another Bottle. Again, if they knock down more than the one Bottle, Number Two must reset any others upright.

Number Two then runs back to the pony and before crossing the Centre Line remounts. With Number One leading the pony, Number Two and Number One ride/run back over the Start/Finish Line.

Riders Numbers Three and Four repeat the actions of Numbers One and Two.

The winning Team is the one whose Numbers Four riding and Number Three leading the pony are first over the Start/Finish Line.

If a Team completely runs out of Boules, the rider concerned must run forward with the Bucket to collect any number and then continue the race from behind the Changeover Line as before.

Ponies must be led by the nearer rein throughout. If contact is lost, leader and pony must return to the point that the contact was lost before continuing. The white hat band is worn by the Number Four rider who is on the pony when crossing the Start/Finish Line.

When bowling/throwing the Boules, the rider's foot must not be touching the Changeover Line.

Line Stewards will move forward and level with the Changeover Line and call 'Fault, throw again' if the rider's foot touches the line.

EVENT 7: Spell STRUK Pole (Junior version) (Race requires 5 members)

A Bending Pole will be set up on the Centre Line in line with the Cartons and Table at the Changeover End.

A Table is placed in the circle 3 metres beyond the Changeover Line. On the Table will be a bucket containing SEVEN Cartons. The Cartons will have the following letters S-T-R-U-K–Blank-Blank.

Number Five will stand behind the Table with the bucket on at the Changeover End. All four riders are mounted at the Start/Finish end.

On the signal to start Number One, carrying a Blank Carton with no letter on it rides to the Bending Pole and slots the Carton over the pole. They then continue to the Changeover End, collect a Blank Carton from Number Five, ride down the arena and slot the Carton over the pole and then ride back to the Changeover End and collect a Blank Carton from Number Five and ride down the arena and hand the Carton to Number Two.

Number Two rides to the Bending Pole and slots the Blank Carton over the pole. They then continue to the Changeover End and collects Carton with the letter K on it from Number Five, rides down the arena and slots the Carton over the pole and then ride back to the Changeover End and collect a Carton with the letter U on it from Number Five and ride down the arena and hand the Carton to Number Three.

Number Three rides to the Bending Pole and slots the Carton (Letter U) over the pole. They then continue to the Changeover End and collects Carton with the letter R on it from Number Five, rides down the arena and slots the Carton over the pole and then ride back to the Changeover End and collect a Carton with the letter T on it from Number Five and ride down the arena and hand the Carton to Number Four.

Number Four rides to the Bending Pole and slots the Carton (Letter T) over the pole. They then continue to the Changeover End and collects the Carton with the letter S on it from Number Five, rides down the arena and slots the Carton over the pole and then crosses the Start/Finish Line.

The winning team is the one whose Number Four is first over the Start/Finish Line and with all Cartons on the pole reading from top to bottom S, T, R, U, K, Blank, Blank, Blank.

Cartons placed in the wrong order, or the wrong way up, must be corrected by the rider concerned, the narrow neck of each Carton is deemed as being the top.

Number Five must remain behind the Table at the Changeover End. They may move to retrieve a piece of dropped equipment but must return to their position behind the Table before continuing their role in the race.

EVENT 8: EGUK 5 Flag

The details of this game are set out in Prince Philip Cup (Senior) Zone Games, Event number 10.

SPARE: 2 Mug

The details of this game are set out in Prince Philip Cup (Senior) Area Games, Event number 7.

29.   PAIRS ZONE GAMES 2025

EVENT 1: Concierge Medical Post Box (Pairs)

A Bending Pole topped with a Penny Dish will be set up level with Pole 1.

On the Centre Line will be a Post Box with its feet astride the Centre Line and 3 metres behind the Changeover Line will be a Table on which there are two Brochures.

Both riders are mounted at the Start/Finish End.

On the signal to start Number One, carrying a Coin (10cm in diameter), will ride to place the Coin in the Penny Dish. They then ride across the Changeover Line, collect a Brochure from the Table, ride back to the Post Box and post the Brochure through so that it drops on the ground on the Start/Finish side of the Post Box. This must be done by pushing the Brochure through from the side of the Post Box nearer the Changeover Line and not by pulling from the other side. They then ride to collect the Coin from the Penny Dish and hand it to Number Two behind the Start/Finish

Line.

Number Two will complete the race in the same way. The winning Pair will be the one whose Number Two is first over the Start/Finish Line carrying the Coin.

If the Post Box is knocked over, the rider concerned must replace it. If the Post Box is knocked from its original position, providing the Post Box feet are astride the Centre Line (as per original start position), or at least one foot is touching the Centre Line the rider may continue. The Brochure must not be folded at any time during the race. The rider must make a genuine attempt to post the Brochure while mounted but provided they have done so, if they drop the Brochure they may dismount and post it unmounted

Equipment information – At Zone Finals and at the Pony Club Championships the following size Post Boxes will be used.

Height – 122cm (to slot 94 cm)

Width - 41cm

Slot opening - 3cm x 25cm

Brochure - A4 brochures, 1cm thick, in plastic sleeve or wallet

EVENT 2: Tennis Ball Shuffle (Pairs)

A pole topped with a "socket" containing a tennis ball placed in the 9 O'clock position as viewed from the Start/Finish Line is placed on the Centre Line. Ball cones are placed level with Poles 1 and 4.

Numbers One is mounted at the Start/Finish End and Numbers Two at the Changeover End.

On the signal to start Number One, carrying a tennis ball, rides to and places the tennis ball on the cone level with Pole 1. They then ride to the "socket", remove the tennis ball, ride to and place the tennis ball on the cone level with Pole 4 before crossing the Changeover Line.

Number Two rides to the cone level with Pole 4 collects the tennis ball and places this in the "socket" at any position. They then ride to the cone level with Pole 1, remove the tennis ball and carry it across the Start/Finish Line.

EVENT 3: Hollywood Bowl Bowling (Pairs)

Four full-sized, weighted Bottles with 500 grams in each will be placed 30 centimetres apart 3 metres beyond the Changeover Line.

A Bucket with 12 weighted, plastic "Boules" will be placed in front of the Changeover Line.

Numbers One and Two with one pony will form up, on foot, behind the Start/Finish Line, each facing forward and on the near side of the pony. On the signal to start, Number One mounts the pony. This must be done befor crossing the Start/Finish Line. Number Two then leads the pony across the Centre Line. Number One dismounts after the Centre Line and Number Tw waits holding the pony.

Whilst Number Two holds the pony, Number One runs to the Bucket and from behind the Changeover Line bowls/throws a Boule at the Bottles. They must knock down two Bottles, even if this is done using just one Boule. If they knock down more than two Bottles, Number One must reset any others upright. Number One runs to the pony and whilst Number One holds the pony, Number Two runs to the Bucket and from behind the Changeover Line bowls/throws a Boule(s) to knock down the other two Bottles. even if this is done using just one Boule. Number Two then runs back to the pony and mounts and Number One leads and runs with the pony leading on either side of the pony. Number Two must be mounted before crossing the Centre Line. The Pair ride/run down the arena and across the Start/Finish Line.

If a Pair completely runs out of Boules, the rider concerned must run forward with the Bucket to collect any number of Boules and then continu the race from behind the Changeover Line as before.

The pony must be led by the nearer rein throughout. The white hat band is worn by the rider who throws the last Boule.

When bowling/throwing the Boules, the rider's foot must not be touching the line. Line Stewards will move forward and level with the changeover line and call 'Fault, throw again' if the rider's foot touches the Changeover Line. If they knock down a Bottle with their foot touching the line, they mus replace the Bottle upright before throwing/bowling again.

EVENT 4: Tally Ho Farm Tack Shop (Pairs)

The details of this game are set out in Pairs Area Games, Event number 5

EVENT 5: Rope (Pairs)

Lines of four Bending Poles will be erected approximately 7 to 9 metres apart.

Number One, carrying a rope approximately 90cm in length, is mounted a the Start/Finish End and Number Two is mounted at the Changeover End. The rope must not be looped or knotted throughout the race. Holding of hands during the race is not permitted.

On the signal to start, Number One will ride up the arena weaving through the Bending Poles to cross the Changeover Line, where Number Two will grasp the rope and both riders return through the Bending Poles and over the Start/Finish Line. Both riders must have hold of the rope before crossing back into the field of play at the Changeover Line.

The winning Pair will be the one who cross the Start/Finish Line first, mounted and carrying the rope between them.

Should either rider let go of the rope at any time when in the field of play, the Pair must go back and resume the race from the point where the fault occurred.

EVENT 6: Spell STRUK Pole (Pairs)

A Bending Pole will be set up level with Pole 1 with three blank Cartons already placed on the pole and in line with a circle 3 metres behind the Changeover Line.

In the circle 3 metres beyond the Changeover Line will be placed randomly FOUR individually marked Cartons. The Cartons will have the following letters S-T-R-U.

On the signal to start Number One, carrying a Carton with letter K on it rides to the Bending Pole and slots the Carton over the pole. Number One continues to the changeover end, dismounts and collects the Carton with the letter U, rides down the arena and slots the Carton over the pole. They then ride back up the arena to the Changeover End, dismount and collect the Carton with the letter R on it, remount, ride down the arena and hand the Carton to Number Two behind the Start/Finish Line.

Number Two rides to the Bending Pole and slots the Carton (Letter R) over the pole. They then continue to the Changeover End, dismount and collect the Carton with the letter T, remount, ride down the arena and slots this Carton over the pole and then rides back to the Changeover End, dismounts and collects the Carton with the letter S on it, remount, rides down the arena and slots the Carton over the pole and then crosses the Start/Finish Line.

The winning Pair is the one whose Number Two is first over the Start/Finish Line and with all Cartons on the pole reading from top to bottom S, T, R, U, K, Blank, Blank, Blank.

Cartons placed in the wrong order, or the wrong way up, must be corrected by the rider concerned, the narrow neck of each Carton is deemed as being the top.

Cartons kicked out of the circle by a pony should be replaced by the Line Steward concerned. If a Carton is knocked into the field of play and cannot be retrieved safely by the Line Steward, the rider collecting that Carton must pick it up and carry it over the Changeover Line before mounting and continuing the race.

EVENT 7: Three-Legged Sack (Pairs)

Number One will be mounted behind the Start/Finish Line and Number Two will be mounted behind the Changeover Line.

On the signal to start Number One, carrying a sack, rides down the arena, over the Changeover Line and dismounts. Number Two dismounts when Number One has crossed the Changeover Line. Numbers One and Two each put one leg into the sack. Holding the sack in one hand and leading their ponies with the other, they run back together over the Start/Finish Line.

The winning Pair will be the one who are first over the Start/Finish line.

The sack may be handed to Number Two before Number One has dismounted providing the incoming pony's feet have fully crossed the Changeover Line. Ponies must be led by the nearer rein. The top of the sack must not be rolled over at the start of the race.

EVENT 8: Sword (Pairs)

A line of four Bending Poles will be erected approximately 7 to 9 metres apart for each team. A plastic sword ring with a 100mm diameter hole will be placed on each of the four poles secured with an elastic band. On Poles and 2 the stem of the rings by which the ring is secured will be on the back edge of the Bending Pole and on Poles 3 and 4 it will be on the front edge of the Bending Pole.

Number One will be mounted behind the Start/Finish Line and Number Two will be mounted behind the Changeover Line.

On the signal to start Number One holding a Sword rides up the arena, collects two rings from the top of any poles using the Sword, rides over the Changeover Line and passes the Sword with the rings still on to Number Two. Number Two rides down the arena, collects the final two rings from t top of the poles using the Sword and rides over the Start/Finish Line.

The winning Pair is the one whose Number Two crosses the Start/Finish Line first holding the Sword with all four rings on it.

The Sword must always be held behind the cross bar on the Sword and no part of the hand/finger shall be in front of the cross bar throughout the race.

Should a ring be knocked off a pole, or should a ring be dropped, the rider may dismount and pick it up by hand and may hold any part of the Sword. They may hold any rings on the Sword with their fingers to help collect any other rings and must go back to where the error took place and continue the race holding the Sword behind the cross bar. To help with remounting the rider may place the Sword against a pole and pick up the Sword by the blade when mounted but must go back to where the error took place and continue the race holding the Sword behind the cross bar.

If during a handover the Sword or rings are dropped, providing a genuine attempt has been made to handover, Number One may dismount and collect the Sword and rings and still being dismounted can hand the Sword to Number Two providing they hand over the Sword with their hand behind the cross bar.

If the Sword or rings are dropped over the Changeover Line and no genuine attempt has been made to handover the Sword to Number Two, then Number One may dismount and pick up the dropped Sword and/or rings but must remount and hand over the Sword to Number Two mounted and must do so with their hand behind the cross bar.

At a changeover, if the rings are dropped into the field of play by Number Two, they must correct the error and re-cross the Changeover Line before completing the race.

There is no penalty should a pole be knocked down.

EVENT 9: PGUK 3 Mug (Pairs)

Four Bending Poles are placed in a line 7 to 9 metres apart. Mugs are placed on Poles 2, 3 and 4.

Both riders are mounted at the Start/Finish End. On the signal to start Number One rides down the arena, moves the Mug from Pole 2 to Pole 1, then the Mug from Pole 3 to Pole 2, then the Mug from Pole 4 to Pole 3 and then rides back over the Start/Finish Line.

Number Two then rides down the arena, moves the Mug from Pole 3 to Pole 4, then the Mug from Pole 2 to Pole 3, then the Mug from Pole 1 to Pole 2 and then rides back over the Start/Finish line.

Mugs must be placed on each Pole in the correct order. Should one fall or is missed the rider must replace the Mug before continuing. If the next Mug has already been moved, then the rider must replace this Mug on the Pole from which they took it before correcting the first error.

The winning Pair is the one whose Number Two is first over the Start/Finish line with Mugs on Poles 2, 3 and 4.

EVENT 10: EGUK 5 Flag (Pairs)

A Flag Cone will be placed 3 metres behind the Changeover Line and another on the Centre Line. Each pair will have five Flags on canes. Four of these will be in the Pair's Flag Cone on the Centre Line and one will be carried by Number One at the start.

Both riders are mounted at the Start/Finish End. On the signal to start, Number One rides to the other end of the arena and places the Flag they are carrying in the Flag Cone behind the Changeover Line. Number One then rides back, picks another Flag from the Flag Cone on the Centre Line and rides back up the arena to place a second Flag into the Flag Cone behind the Changeover Line. Number One then collects a Flag from the Flag Cone on the Centre Line and hands this Flag to Number Two behind the Start/Finish Line.

Number Two will complete the race in the same way up and down the arena so that, at the end, the Pair will have placed four Flags in the Flag Cone behind the Changeover Line and Number Two finishes over the Start/Finish Line mounted and carrying the fifth Flag.

Should the Flag Cone be knocked over, the rider must put it up again, replacing any Flags there may have been in it. Should a rider take more than one Flag from the Flag Cone, they must replace the surplus. They may dismount to correct mistakes.

The winning Pair is the one whose Number Two is first over the Start/Finish Line carrying a Flag and with four Flags in the Flag Cone behind the Changeover Line.

If the flag should come off the cane, the cane may be used to complete the race.

On windy days rubber bands can be used to keep the flags furled and prevent them blowing together.

SPARE: 2 Mug (Pairs)

The details of this game are set out in Pairs Area Games, Event number 7.

APPENDICES

APPENDIX A – PLAN OF ARENA

1. Arena Size – including collecting ring 125m X 74m.

2. Manned ropes should be used to open and close the entrance and exit at the start and finish of each race. In games where equipment or the fifth member is positioned 3m beyond the Changeover line, a circle (45cm diameter) should be marked on the ground.

KEY

CB Commentator's Box   ***** Bending Posts   **X** Corner marker posts
+ Centre of lane markers for non-bending events

The large X shows the position of the flags on each corner of the Start/Finish Line and Changeover Line and defines 'The Field of Play'.

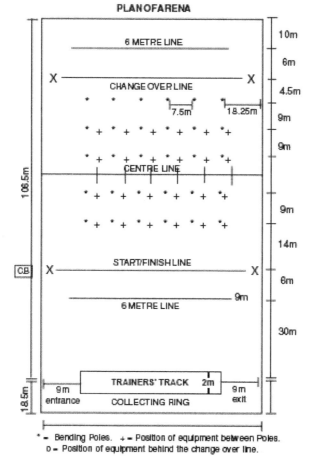

PLAN OF ARENA

* = Bending Poles.   + = Position of equipment between Poles.
o = Position of equipment behind the change over line.

APPENDIX B – MOUNTED GAMES EQUIPMENT – ALPHABETICAL

These are the minimum requirements and spares should be available in case of loss or breakage.

Recommended items of equipment for Area and Zone Competitions (all sizes are approximate)

Quantities are per lane used – multiply by the number of lanes needed for the competition.

Bending

► 5 bending poles - Poles should be between 3cm and 3.5cm diameter, 1.4m high
► 1 baton - 2.5cm in diameter and 30cm long

Concierge Medical Bandage and First Aid Bin (Sock & Bucket)

► 5 crepe cotton bandages, approx. 10cm x 4cm, taped
► 1 bucket (white bucket branded with Concierge Medical label and first aid cross in blue)

Concierge Medical Bandage and First Aid Bin (Sock & Bucket) (Junior)

► 5 crepe cotton bandages, approx. 10cm x 4cm, taped
► 1 bucket (white bucket branded with Concierge Medical label and first aid cross in blue)
► 1 bending pole
► 1 penny dish

Concierge Medical Bandage and First Aid Bin (Sock and Bucket) (Pairs)

► 3 crepe cotton bandages, approx. 10cm x 4cm, taped
► 1 bucket (white bucket branded with Concierge Medical label and first aid cross in blue)

Concierge Medical Post Box

► 1 post box - Height 122cm (to slot 94cm). Width 41cm. Slot opening 3cm x 25cm
► 1 bending pole
► 1 penny dish
► 1 coin - 10cm diameter
► 4 Concierge Medical brochures – A4 brochures, 1cm thick, in plastic sleeve or wallet

Concierge Medical Post Box (Pairs)

- 1 post box - Height 122cm (to slot 94cm). Width 41cm. Slot opening 3cm x 25cm
- 1 bending pole
- 1 penny dish
- 1 coin - 10cm diameter
- 2 Concierge Medical brochures – A4 brochures, 1cm thick, in plastic sleeve or wallet
- 1 table

EGUK 2 Mug

- 4 bending poles
- 2 mugs

EGUK 5 Flag

- 2 Flag Cones - 32cm high, 10cm diameter hole in top
- 5 flags - 1.25m long consisting of good quality bamboo or plastic canes with flags firmly fixed, flags to be 23cm square or triangular

Four Flag

- 3 Flag Cones – 32cm high, 10cm diameter hole in top
- 4 flags - 1.25m long consisting of good quality bamboo or plastic canes with flags firmly fixed, flags to be 23cm square or triangular

Hollywood Bowl Ball and Cone

- 2 ball cones - 50cm high, aperture at the top 4.5cm diameter to balance ball on
- 2 tennis balls

Hollywood Bowl Bending (Juniors)

- 5 bending poles – Poles should be between 3cm and 3.5cm diameter, 1.4m high
- 1 baton – 2.5cm in diameter and 30cm long

Hollywood Bowl Bowling

- 4 bottles - Senior size weighing 500g
- 1 bucket
- 12 boules

PG Sports Pyramid (Spell PGUK)

- ► 2 tables
- ► 1 plastic box with the letter 'P' on each side
- ► 1 plastic box with the letter 'G' on each side
- ► 1 plastic box with the letter 'U' on each side
- ► 1 plastic box with the letter 'K' on each side
- ► (plastic boxes are approx. 18cm square, 10cm deep and weighted with sand/sawdust to 500g)

PG Sports Rosette Row

- ► 1 bin
- ► 1 gibbet
- ► 1 cane with a hook on the end and a rubber stopper 10cm from the hook
- ► 1 blue aluminium composite rosette with the letter 'P' on each side
- ► 1 red aluminium composite rosette with the letter 'G' on each side
- ► 1 green aluminium composite rosette with the letter 'U' on each side
- ► 1 yellow aluminium composite rosette with the letter 'K' on each side

PG Sports Rosette Row (Junior)

- ► 1 table
- ► 1 gibbet
- ► 1 blue aluminium composite rosette with the letter 'P' on each side
- ► 1 red aluminium composite rosette with the letter 'G' on each side
- ► 1 green aluminium composite rosette with the letter 'U' on each side
- ► 1 yellow aluminium composite rosette with the letter 'K' on each side

PGUK 3 Mug (Pairs)

- ► 4 bending poles
- ► 3 mugs

Rope

- ► 4 bending poles
- ► 1 rope - 90cm long

Spell STRUK Pole

- ► 1 bending pole
- ► 8 plastic cartons - 3 blank cartons and the others with the letters S, T, U, K on them. Cartons are approx. 5cm diameter at the top and 15cm tall

Spell STRUK Pole (Junior)

- ▸ 1 bending pole
- ▸ 8 plastic cartons - 3 blank cartons and the others with the letters S, T, R, U, K on them. Cartons are approx. 5cm diameter at the top and 15cm tall
- ▸ 1 table
- ▸ 1 bucket

Sword

- ▸ 4 bending poles
- ▸ 4 plastic sword rings with a 10cm diameter hole in the middle
- ▸ 1 sword
- ▸ Elastic bands

Tally Ho Farm Tack Shop

- ▸ 1 bending pole
- ▸ 1 penny dish
- ▸ 1 coin - 10cm diameter
- ▸ 1 plastic grooming tray
- ▸ 2 tables
- ▸ 1 tail bandage
- ▸ 1 dandy brush
- ▸ 1 rubber curry comb
- ▸ 1 tin of saddle soap or shoe polish

Tennis Ball Shuffle

- ▸ 2 ball cones - 50cm high, aperture at the top 4.5cm diameter to balance ball on
- ▸ 1 bending pole
- ▸ 1 socket board
- ▸ 2 tennis balls

Three-legged Sack

- ▸ 1 hessian sack approx. 100cm x 63cm

Two Flag

- ▸ 2 Flag Cones - 32cm high, 10cm diameter hole in top
- ▸ 2 flags - 1.25m long consisting of good quality bamboo or plastic canes with flags firmly fixed, flags to be 23cm square or triangular

Tyre

- 1 motorcycle tyre – approx. 45cm x 7cm

STARTER'S FLAG

1 White Flag approximately 30cm x 30cm, on a cane.

LINE STEWARD BOARDS

12 Square boards, numbered in pairs 1-6 measuring 20cm x 20cm with a narrow piece attached to the back measuring 50cm (with 20cm over hanging forming the handle) – see below.

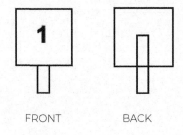

FRONT   BACK

CLOTHING

Licensed Suppliers who are permitted to print The Pony Club logo can be found on The Pony Club website: https://pcuk.org/licensed-suppliers/

APPENDIX C – DIRECTIONS FOR ORGANISERS

These directions apply specifically to Area competitions and higher, but they can also serve as a useful guideline for all Mounted Games competitions when applicable.

ADMINISTRATION

It is essential that Organisers have thorough knowledge of the whole Mounted Games Rulebook.

LINE STEWARDS

A list of Line Stewards should be provided to the Official Steward prior to the briefing. Close collaboration with the Area Line Steward Co-ordinator (if appointed) or Organiser is crucial.

LAYOUT OF SHOWGROUND

The arena size is 125m x 74m (see Appendix A). A "6m line" will be positioned behind the Start and Changeover lines. Approximately six people should set up the arena in a morning and metal posts must not be used. Other essential requirements include:

- First Aid cover
- Signage for roads
- Horsebox parking
- Accessible water
- Secretary's tent (horsebox or trailer can be used)
- Public address system (must be tested before the first event)
- Scoreboard
- Toilet facilities including an accessible toilet
- Commentator's box (should align with the Start/Finish line)
- Public refreshment outlet
- Lunch area for judges/officials

TECHNICAL RACE EQUIPMENT

If Organisers already have some different, but equally suitable, equipment, this may be used. Teams must be informed at least one month prior to the competition to facilitate practice.

SPONSORSHIP

Any sponsorship should be tasteful and aligned with The Pony Club's image and brand guidelines.

PROGRAMME

Any programmes or information sent to competitors of the event should include:

- ▸ List of events
- ▸ Timetable
- ▸ Participating Teams and their colours
- ▸ Score sheet
- ▸ Names of the Organiser and Official Steward

SECRETARY

The Secretary should handle rosettes, and catering arrangements. They should also collect Declaration Forms, checking passports and vaccinations for the Official Steward's verification before the briefing. The most current Vaccination Policy can be found on The Pony Club website.

FIRST AID REQUIREMENTS

Refer to the current Health and Safety Rulebook for the First Aid and Veterinary Matrix. If a veterinary surgeon cannot attend, ensure one is on call with a noted contact number at the Secretary's tent. They should be located near the ring, with a tarpaulin available for emergencies.

FARRIER

The Organiser should arrange for a Farrier to be present or on call.

GATE/PARKING STEWARD

They are responsible for directing vehicle parking.

ROSETTES

For Area Competitions, rosettes are ordered by the Organiser, and as a minimum, the following should be awarded for final placings:

- ▸ Up to 8 entries: 1st – 4th
- ▸ Up to 10 entries: up to 5th
- ▸ Over 10 entries: up to 6th
- ▸ Turnout rosettes 1st – 3rd

It is recommended that all Team Members receive a rosette. At Zone and Championship Competitions, rosettes will be awarded to all five riding members and the sixth non-riding reserve from each team, supplied by The Pony Club Office.

TURNOUT COMPETITION

Teams will be inspected in their competition attire before the event. Branches must be notified in advance of inspection times, ideally scheduling them at five-minute intervals. Team Trainers must be present during inspections, but if it coincides with the Briefing, they can appoint a substitute. Teams will parade before the competition starts, and rosettes will be awarded to the top three Teams.

REPORT TO THE PONY CLUB OFFICE

After the competition, the Organiser must provide the Official Steward with:

- A marked-up score sheet for Prince Philip Cup, Junior and Pairs Team Competitions
- All Declaration Forms
- A report on any issues and suggestions for future improvements.
- Recommendation for any Teams not automatically qualified who would be suitable or not suitable for an Additional Qualification.

The above should all be sent as scanned copies by email, or a hard copy by post to The Pony Club Office. Once it has been confirmed by the Sports Officer that all Declaration Forms have been received, original hard copies should be destroyed.

NOTICE TO TEAMS

Inform Teams of:

- Venue and directions
- Times of Declaration, Briefing, Turnout Inspection, and first event.
- Technical equipment details, if different from Appendix B.
- Catering provisions
- Organiser contact details, including mobile number for the event day

The Organiser must also promptly inform the Official Steward of all arrangements and seek advice for any issues.

APPENDIX D – THE OFFICIAL STEWARD – DUTIES

The Official Steward for Area competitions and above, appointed by The Pony Club Office, ensures compliance with all rules and holds final authority over the event. Their key responsibilities include inspecting and approving the arena layout and equipment prior to the competition.

They conduct the briefing, supervising Line Stewards and assigning their positions. An experienced Line Steward will be appointed to handle objections, and this steward must raise their board immediately upon receiving any objection, refraining from discussion.

The Official Steward is responsible for reporting infringements to the Chief Judge and coordinating with First Aid personnel regarding their placement and when to summon assistance. They enforce concussion rules as outlined in the Health and Safety Rulebook (see pcuk.org) and adjudicate objections, referring unresolved matters to The Pony Club Office if necessary.

In cases of serious rule breaches, the Official Steward may consider disqualification, consulting with the Organiser and any present Mounted Games Committee member before making a decision.

To effectively manage the competition, the Official Steward must have a height-measuring stick, scales (bathroom scales are acceptable), and a whistle readily available to stop the race if required. At the end of the day, they will thank the Organiser on behalf of the Mounted Games Committee.

After the competition, the Official Steward must promptly submit a marked-up Score Sheet (for the Prince Philip Cup, Junior, and Pairs Team Competitions), Declaration Forms for all Teams, and a report outlining any difficulties encountered along with suggestions for future improvements. They must also ensure that they, or someone they appoint, uploads the results to Pony Club Results.

APPENDIX E – BRIEFING

The Official Steward conducts the Briefing at least one hour before the first event, ideally in a covered area. Punctual attendance is essential for all required.

Preparation:

- The Official Steward should have received all Declaration Forms for verification before the Briefing.

- A list of Line Stewards should also be submitted.

Attendance: The Official Steward will confirm presence of required attendees, who should include:

- District Commissioners or their representatives

- Team Trainers

- All Line Stewards

- The Judges (x2)

- The Starter

- Line Steward Co-ordinator (if appointed)

During the Briefing:

- Ensure all questions and answers are audible.

- Verify that all Line Stewards and the Starter understand their duties as per APPENDIX F.

- Explain the signalling procedure, stressing that Line Stewards must NOT call back or warn competitors.

Objection Handling: An experienced Line Steward will receive objections on the far side of the arena. Upon receiving an objection, they must raise their board immediately and not engage in discussion.

Additional Reminders:

- Start/Finish Line Stewards will distribute and collect necessary equipment (e.g., batons).

- Changeover Line Stewards are responsible for equipment at the far end of the arena.

- ▸ Clarify the use of the Starter's whistle for false starts and remind Line Stewards not to oversee their own Team, stressing focus during races.

Rules Overview:

- ▸ Summarise key General Rules and any specific points for each race.

- ▸ Explain the rules on objections, stating that objections regarding starting, judging, or stewarding decisions are not permitted.

Before briefing the Judges and Starter, other attendees may leave.

Judges Briefing: The Judges must be positioned together at the same end of the start/finish line as the commentator for effective communication. They are responsible for placing competitors as they finish but should not concern themselves with any infringements. During Zone Finals and Championships, Judges will consult with the Official Steward regarding any Start/Finish line infringements.

The Judges will record the placings of all Teams for potential eliminations. The Official Steward should clarify the finishing procedures for each race.

Pre-Competition Notes: Briefing Notes may be sent by the Official Steward/Organiser before the competition.

APPENDIX F – INSTRUCTIONS FOR LINE STEWARDS AND THE STARTER AT AREA COMPETITIONS

Line Stewards

1. Purpose of Signals: Line steward signals are intended for the guidance of the Official Steward, not for the competitors.

2. Knowledge Requirements: Line Stewards must have a thorough understanding of the rules and details of each race they will oversee. They should have Line Stewarded at least two Team practices or competitions prior to their assigned event and must be at least 18 years old.

3. Attendance at Briefing: Line Stewards are required to attend the Briefing, which takes place at least one hour before the first event. Punctuality is essential.

4. Team Composition:

▸ Each Team will have two Line Stewards.

▸ One Line Steward should stand 3-4 metres behind the Changeover line, aligned with their designated lane.

▸ The second Line Steward will be positioned at the side of the arena as directed by the Official Steward.

▸ For events with six Teams, Line Stewards for lanes 1, 2, and 3 will be on the starter's side, while those for lanes 4, 5, and 6 will be on the opposite side. They must maintain a distance apart to monitor changeovers effectively.

▸ Each Line Steward should have a numbered board and, if possible, wear a fluorescent bib for visibility.

5. Conflict of Interest: Line Stewards should avoid officiating in heats or finals involving their own Team, if possible.

6. Signalling Infringements: Any rule infringement must be signalled immediately by raising the numbered board high and keeping it up until the end of the race, unless the issue is resolved, in which case it should be lowered promptly.

7. Coordinated Signalling: When one Line Steward signals an infringement, the Line Steward at the opposite end must signal at the same time.

8. Obstruction Protocol: If a Team causes obstruction, the Line Steward for that Team does not signal until the end of the race. At that point, they will raise their board for the Official Steward's attention. The Line Steward for the obstructed Team does not signal.

9. Communication Restrictions: Line Stewards must not call back or instruct competitors. However, the Changeover Line Steward may briefly answer any questions from competitors.

10. Changeover Line: Line Stewards at the Changeover Line must ensure that competitors do not ride back down the arena until the race has concluded.

11. Equipment Management: If a Team's equipment is disrupted by another Team, the nearest Line Steward should assist in setting it up again if it is safe to do so.

12. Focus and Distraction: Line Stewards must maintain close concentration throughout each race and avoid distractions, including any incidents in other lanes. Mobile phones should be turned off and not used during the competition.

13. Safety Discretion: If equipment appears broken and dangerous, the Line Steward may raise their board. Note that the race will not be re-run under such circumstances (see General Rules).

14. Rider Positioning: Only the next rider should occupy their position on the Start or Changeover Line; all others must remain behind the 6m line (see General Rules).

15. Loose Ponies: If a pony runs loose, the Line Stewards of the affected Team may attempt to catch it, but only after it has exited the 'playing area'.

16. Start Position Responsibility: Line Stewards are not responsible for positioning the ponies at the start.

17. Attendance Obligation: Line Stewards from a Branch Team must still attend the Area Meeting, even if their Team is withdrawn from the competition, unless otherwise notified by the Organiser.

18. Reporting Issues: Line Stewards must report to the Official Steward any person who questions their decisions, is abusive, or obstructs their duties in any way.

The Starter

The Official Steward must confirm the Starter's position and ensure proper flag usage, with the Starter's whistle readily available for false starts.

1. Experience: The Starter must have experience in Mounted Games competitions.

2. Positioning: The Starter should stand in line with the first bending pole, on the same side as the Judges, ensuring visibility for all competitors.

3. Unruly Ponies: If a pony becomes unruly, the Starter or Official Steward will instruct it to move behind the 6m line.

4. False Starts: In case of a false start, the Starter will blow the whistle and raise the flag to recall the Teams.

5. Starting Procedure:

   ▶ Raise the flag upright while riders settle, keeping the whistle in the other hand.

   ▶ Lower the flag AWAY FROM the riders when they are stationary. Avoid excessive movements that may unsettle ponies.

   ▶ Discourage riders from raising their hands; remind them that they are visible and should maintain two hands on the reins.

6. Consultation: The Starter should consult the Official Steward if any doubts arise.

APPENDIX G – HEAD INJURY AND CONCUSSION FLOWCHART

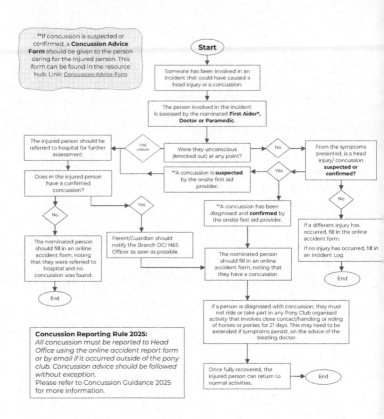

**If concussion is suspected or confirmed, a Concussion Advice Form should be given to the person caring for the Injured person. This form can be found in the resource hub. Link: Concussion-Advice-Form

Start

Someone has been involved in an incident that could have caused a head injury or a concussion.

The person involved in the incident is assessed by the nominated **First Aider*, Doctor or Paramedic.**

Were they unconscious (knocked out) at any point?

From the symptoms presented, is a head injury/ concussion **suspected or confirmed?**

Yes/unsure — The injured person should be referred to hospital for further assessment.

Does in the injured person have a confirmed concussion?

No — The nominated person should fill in an online accident form, noting that they were referred to hospital and no concussion was found.

End

Yes — Parent/Guardian should notify the Branch DC/ H&S Officer as soon as possible.

No — **A concussion is **suspected** by the onsite first aid provider.

Yes — **A concussion has been diagnosed and **confirmed** by the onsite first aid provider.

The nominated person should fill in an online accident form, noting that they have a concussion.

No — If a different injury has occurred, fill in the online accident form.

If no injury has occurred, fill in an Incident Log.

End

If a person is diagnosed with concussion, they must not ride or take part in any Pony Club organised activity that involves close contact/handling or riding of horses or ponies for 21 days. This may need to be extended if symptoms persist, on the advice of the treating doctor.

Once fully recovered, the injured person can return to normal activities.

End

Concussion Reporting Rule 2025:
All concussion must be reported to Head Office using the online accident report form or by email if it occurred outside of the pony club. Concussion advice should be followed without exception.
Please refer to Concussion Guidance 2025 for more information.

---

* If concussion is diagnosed by a first aider, this diagnosis can only be overruled by a doctor and letter evidence will be required.

If you need any advice or support, please contact the Safety Team Safety@PCUK.org

APPENDIX H – GUIDE TO ORGANISING THE TACK AND TURNOUT COMPETITION

It is recommended that the Organiser of any Prince Philip Competition understands how to organise a Tack and Turnout Competition – if the tack and turnout takes a long time, the whole day can be disrupted.

We advise Organisers to allocate three Judges and a writer to the tack and turnout section, they can each be given specific job, i.e.

▸ Judge 1 can check the pony.

▸ Judge 2 can check the tack.

▸ Judge 3 can check the rider.

The writer helps to make the job for the Judges a little easier.

Please note that all the Judges should be up to date with the current Tack and Turnout rules and have a rule book to hand.

Before the competition it is advised to create a timetable allocating the time which each Team must present to the Tack and Turnout Judges, these timetables can be posted to Teams beforehand.

Allow each Team approximately 5 minutes to be checked and judged. Additionally, try to allow some additional time before the parade in case there are any issues that need to be referred to the Official Steward.

If a Team presents a 6th Member at Tack and Turnout, they are checked but their score is not noted.

APPENDIX I – AREA COORDINATOR GUIDELINES

Main areas of focus for Area Coordinators:

1. To give support to the Official Steward at the Area Mounted Games competition.

2. To respond to any branch or request for help in starting up Mounted Games or a branch or request to give some initial help with grass roots and novice Teams, riders and their Team trainer.

3. Work with the Area Representative and Branches and in the Area to enable them to offer Mounted Games. This should be done by being a source of advice and support to help understanding of the game and by helping them find coaches and equipment.

4. Support the development of Mounted Games within the Area. To help promote branches and to start up grass roots & novice 'Give it a Go' taster Rallies and fun training days.

5. Where possible, to help branches to organise Area training events which are open to all Pony Club members from within the Area.

6. Act as a point of contact within the Area for Parents, Guardians, members and Branches who want to know about the sport of Mounted Games and opportunities to play it.

FIXTURES FOR 2025

REGIONAL STUDY DAYS

See up-to-date lists on the pcuk.org website.

- Saturday 4th January – Central England – RDA National Training Centre, CV35 7AX
- Saturday 1st February – Northern England – Myerscough Equestrian Centre, PR3 0RY
- Saturday 8th February - Area 12 – BCA, Hall Place, SL6 6QR
- Saturday 1st March – Southern Areas – Kingston Maurward, DT2 8PY

TRIALS FOR THE DAKS HOME INTERNATIONAL COMPETITION

- Northern Ireland – 22nd February - Danescroft Equestrian Centre, BT27 5NW
- Wales – 2nd March - Dyffryn Farm Berriew
- England – 8th March – Dallas Burston Polo Grounds
- Scotland – 16th March – Morris Equestrian

DAKS HOME INTERNATIONAL COMPETITION

Royal Windsor Horse Show from 15th to 18th May

ZONE FINALS

- Southern Zone – 5th July – Southfield House, Somerset, BA11 3JY
  Areas: 10 / 13 / 14 / 15 / 16 / 18
- Northern Zone – 5th July – Overton Farm, Crossford, Carluke
  Areas: 1 / 2 / 17 / 19
- Central Zone – 19th & 20th July Stanford Hall, Leicestershire.
  Saturday – Areas: 6 / 8 / 9 / 11 / 12
  Sunday – Areas: 3 / 4 / 5 / 7

THE JCB PONY CLUB CHAMPIONSHIPS 2025 - Offchurch Bury, Offchurch, Leamington Spa, Warwickshire, CV33 9AW

- Junior Championships - Friday 8th August
- Intermediate & Pairs Championships – Saturday 9th August
- Senior Runners-Up Competitions – Sunday 10th August

PRINCE PHILIP CUP FINAL - H.O.Y.S.

- Horse of The Year Show at Resort World, Birmingham – 8th to 12th October 2025

PREVIOUS WINNERS

- 1957   North West Kent
- 1958   Cheshire Hunt (North)
- 1959   High Peak Hunt
- 1960   High Peak Hunt (North)
- 1961   Enfield Chace Hunt
- 1962   High Peak Hunt (North)
- 1963   Angus
- 1964   Atherstone Hunt
- 1965   Blackmore Vale Hunt
- 1966   Woodland
- 1967   Hurworth Hunt
- 1968   Angus
- 1969   Taunton Vale Hunt
- 1970   Atherstone Hunt
- 1971   Atherstone Hunt
- 1972   Strathblane And District
- 1973   Strathblane And District
- 1974   Kirkintilloch And Campsie
- 1975   Peak
- 1976   Wylye Valley Hunt
- 1977   Banwen And District
- 1978   Eglinton Hunt
- 1979   Cheshire Hunt (North)
- 1980   Oakley Hunt
- 1981   Banwen And District
- 1982   Eglinton Hunt
- 1983   Eglinton Hunt
- 1984   Eglinton Hunt
- 1985   Atherstone Hunt
- 1986   Wylye Valley Hunt
- 1987   Eglinton Hunt
- 1988   Eglinton Hunt
- 1989   Oakley Hunt West
- 1990   North Warwickshire
- 1991   Wylye Valley
- 1992   Eglinton Hunt
- 1993   Eglinton Hunt
- 1994   Eglinton Hunt
- 1995   Eglinton Hunt
- 1996   Eglinton Hunt
- 1997   Oakley Hunt West
- 1998   Clydach

- 1999   Poole & District
- 2000   Eglinton Hunt
- 2001   Oakley Hunt West
- 2002   Oakley Hunt West
- 2003   Wylye Valley
- 2004   West Perthshire
- 2005   Eglinton Hunt
- 2006   Banwell
- 2007   Atherstone Hunt
- 2008   Oakley Hunt West
- 2009   Percy Hunt
- 2010   Devon & Somerset
- 2011   Oakley Hunt West
- 2012   Oakley Hunt West
- 2013   Strathearn
- 2014   Warwickshire Hunt
- 2015   Monmouthshire
- 2016   East Kent Hunt
- 2017   Oakley Hunt West
- 2018   West Hants
- 2019   West Hants
- 2020   -
- 2021   West Hants
- 2022   North Herefordshire
- 2023   North Herefordshire
- 2024   North Herefordshire

2025 SPONSORS

With grateful thanks to:

- Hollywood Bowl
- Equestrian Games UK
- PG Sports UK
- STRUK Events
- Concierge Medical
- Tally Ho Farm

Printed in Great Britain
by Amazon